Documenting Learning with ePortfolios

DATE DUE

"*Documenting Learning with ePortfolios: A Guide for College Instructors* is a seminal work. The authors have simply and succinctly captured the present status of ePortfolio work in a manner that is as inclusive as it is comprehensive. More importantly, however, they have illuminated future possibilities in a style that is both pedagogically compelling, easy reading, and extraordinarily informative. Anyone interested in effective online learning should read it."

—Peter Smith, senior vice president, Kaplan Higher Education, author of
Harnessing America's Wasted Talent: A New Ecology of Learning

"Brilliant! A comprehensive resource that links wise practical guidance to a far-reaching vision of the ePortfolio's potential to transform learning and teaching. Invaluable for innovators across higher education, from community colleges to research universities."

—Bret Eynon, Making Connections National Resource Center, LaGuardia
Community College, CUNY

"This book clearly and succinctly explains *why* our students should document their learning, and more importantly, it provides guidance on *how* higher education practitioners can go about it. In a higher education environment steeped in accountability and evidence-based practice, knowing how to have students evidence their capabilities in the digital world is essential for their credibility—and ours!"

—Beverley Oliver, National Teaching Fellow, Australian Learning and Teaching
Council, Curtin University, Australia

Documenting Learning with ePortfolios

▶ A GUIDE FOR COLLEGE INSTRUCTORS

Tracy Penny Light

Helen L. Chen

John C. Ittelson

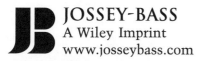
JOSSEY-BASS
A Wiley Imprint
www.josseybass.com

Published by Jossey-Bass
A Wiley Imprint
One Montgomery Street, Suite 1200, San Francisco, CA 94104-4594—www.josseybass.com

Jossey-Bass books and products are available through most bookstores. To contact Jossey-Bass directly call our Customer Care Department within the U.S. at 800-956-7739, outside the U.S. at 317-572-3986, or fax 317-572-4002.

Wiley also publishes its books in a variety of electronic formats and by print-on-demand. Some material included with standard print versions of this book may not be included in e-books or in print-on-demand. If the version of this book that you purchased references media such as CD or DVD that was not included in your purchase, you may download this material at http://booksupport.wiley.com. For more information about Wiley products, visit www.wiley.com.

Library of Congress Cataloging-in-Publication Data
Light, Tracy Penny, 1970-
  Documenting learning with Eportfolios : a guide for college instructors / Tracy Penny Light, Helen L. Chen, John C. Ittelson.
       p. cm.—(Jossey-Bass Higher and Adult Education Series)
   Includes bibliographical references and index.
   ISBN 978-0-470-63620-6 (pbk.); 978-1-118-20494-8 (ebk.); 9978-1-118-20495-5 (ebk.);
978-1-118-20496-2 (ebk.)
   1.   Electronic portfolios in education.   2.   Education, Higher—Computer-assisted instruction.   3.   Education, Higher—Effect of technological innovations on.   I.   Chen, Helen L., 1971- II. Ittelson, John C., 1949- III. Title.
   LB1029.P67L54 2011
   371.33'4—dc23

                                                                      2011039900

Printed in the United States of America
FIRST EDITION

PB Printing   10 9 8 7 6 5 4 3 2

Contents

List of Figures

Preface

Portfolios for teaching and for documenting student work have been around for a long time in a number of fields. For instance, there is a rich heritage of the use of portfolios in both composition and creative writing, in the visual arts, and in architecture. These paper-based portfolios have traditionally been bound volumes or large envelopes or dossiers filled with documents. Although effective mechanisms for showcasing student work, these traditional portfolios were not easily shared among geographically distributed audiences and were limited in scope because of the inability of their owners to easily modify them for different purposes and diverse audiences.

The increasing use of computers in academic settings and the emergence of digital media and the Internet in the 1990s prompted the emergence of new tools which allowed many fields the opportunity to experiment with the concept of electronic learning portfolios (ePortfolios). By the beginning of 2000, portfolios were being expanded and enhanced to include rich media. This was a time when CD-ROMs were the prominent mode of distributing multimedia, audio files, video files, and high-resolution photo images. It was also at about this time that the costs of equipment to capture rich media were coming down; newer equipment was thus becoming widely accessible. Digital video cameras supplanted film cameras; although in the early days video resolution was quite low, the resolution was improving and the cameras themselves were becoming easier to operate. In addition, digital recorders displaced cassette and reel-to-reel audio recorders.

Also in the late 1990s and early 2000s, course management systems (CMSs) were emerging. These systems not only allowed professors to provide their students with electronic versions of handouts and assignments, course syllabi, and calendars, but also offered a means of communicating outside the classroom. These systems clearly provided benefits in traditional classroom settings, but they also offered a new way to move from traditional paper-based correspondence courses or telecourses to what began to emerge in 2000 and 2001—that is, online courses. It was hoped at the time that course management tools coupled with the Internet would create a "sea change," allowing students to attend classes virtually. However, much of the early uses of these systems were simply enhancements of the traditional classroom experience. Now, some ten years later, many colleges are finally offering "blended" or hybrid courses with both a physical and an online presence.

Interest in fully online courses—courses where no physical presence is necessary for either the faculty instructor or the student—is rapidly increasing. With increased bandwidth and various synchronous and asynchronous communication tools, a broader range of students with diverse backgrounds and work experiences can be engaged electronically and can actively take advantage of everything that higher education has to offer. All of these changes have contributed to an environment where technology is ubiquitously integrated into curriculum with ePortfolios representing one of the technology tools now available to support teaching and learning.

In the early days of the ePortfolio movement, there was much discussion about the technology of ePortfolios and their various functionalities and features. In 2002, a series of conversations were held by a consortium of individuals, institutions, and organizations including Dr. Helen Barrett, a pioneer in the field who began her explorations of ePortfolios in teacher education; California State University, Monterey Bay; The Carnegie Foundation for the Advancement of Teaching; Indiana University-Purdue University Indianapolis (IUPUI); Massachusetts Institute of Technology (MIT); Northwestern University; Stanford University; University of Washington; and others which eventually formed the beginnings of EPAC (Electronic Portfolio Action and Communication), a community of practice focusing on ePortfolios broadly defined (see Chen and Ittelson, 2009, for an overview of EPAC). These meetings eventually led to a broader national discussion around both the technological and pedagogical aspects of establishing an ePortfolio culture supported by the American Association for Higher Education (AAHE) and EDUCAUSE's National Learning Infrastructure Initiative (NLII), the predecessor of the EDUCAUSE Learning Initiative. In addition to the EPAC community of practice, these conversations also led to the creation of the Inter/National Coalition for Electronic Portfolio Research (I/NCEPR) in 2004, led by Barbara Cambridge, Darren Cambridge, and Kathleen Yancey, which has convened over sixty campuses in cohorts of ten institutions each to study the impact of ePortfolios on student learning and educational outcomes. There was interest in ePortfolios not only in the United States but also internationally, becoming a truly worldwide initiative with activities taking place in the United Kingdom, the European Union, Canada, New Zealand, and Australia, to name but a few. In fall 2003, the first international conference on ePortfolios was held in France by the EifEL (European Institute for E-Learning) organization in Europe. Six years later, in 2009, the Association for Authentic, Experiential and Evidence-Based Learning (AAEEBL) formed to address and promote educational transformation resulting from new designs in learning and assessment.

Today, ePortfolios are but one approach in a suite of assessment tools that aim to gather evidence of student progress and development in learning outcomes identified at the individual course, program, or institutional level (Leskes and Wright, 2005). As we discuss throughout this book, the first step in identifying how and where ePortfolios can facilitate and support assessment is to establish clear and well-defined learning outcomes. This trend is becoming more prevalent across institutions, as demonstrated by a member survey conducted by the Association of American Colleges and Universities (AAC&U) in April 2009 that found that over three-quarters of the 433 institutional respondents reported having a common set of intended learning outcomes for undergraduates and 96% are either currently assessing or planning for assessment of learning outcomes across the curriculum. Only 4% of these institutions are *not* considering the use of ePortfolios for assessment (Hart Research Associates, 2009).

This groundswell of interest in ePortfolios has fostered increasing connections among the global ePortfolio community including both academic institutions and corporate affiliates. Community practitioners contribute to knowledge transfer around the use of ePortfolios to document learning by conducting research, sharing results, and developing training for faculty instructors and others who are interested in using this approach to assist students to integrate their learning experiences in an engaging and effective manner.

This book provides readers with a "theory-to-practice" approach to the use of ePortfolios for documenting learning. In Part One, we explore the theory behind this pedagogical method for integrative learning, using examples from some of the best practices in ePortfolio thinking today to illustrate the ways in which ePortfolios are being used to engage students. Chapter One explores the rationale behind the need to document learning, situating ePortfolios within the broader context of a changing technological and globalized world. Chapter Two considers the different stakeholders who might be interested in using ePortfolios, either as a tool in itself, or as a means to collect, analyze, and disseminate evidence of student learning. Chapter Three explores a variety of learning, teaching, and assessment activities that can assist with the documentation of learning. In Part Two, we consider the "practice" of creating and implementing ePortfolios by focusing on specific stakeholders. Chapters Four and Five situate ePortfolio practice for students and student affairs practitioners with relevant examples from a variety of campuses. Chapter Six explores ePortfolios and assessment by considering the stakeholders who are interested in ePortfolios for assessment of individual learning as well as at the programmatic or institutional levels. Part Three considers the practical implications for implementing ePortfolios. Chapter Seven explores practical considerations for faculty development initiatives to support ePortfolio initiatives. Chapter Eight focuses on the considerations that need to be taken into account when deciding which technological tools to deploy in support of student learning. Chapter Nine discusses ways to evaluate the impact of ePortfolio initiatives.

Together, these chapters present a framework for thinking about the ways that educators can engage their students in practices that will foster their development into responsible learners and citizens as they document their learning. The intellectual and social development needed in higher education can be facilitated by ePortfolios and we aim to make a compelling and practical case for instructors who wish to implement this pedagogical approach. Finally, we make the case that coherence among the various stakeholders who might be interested in ePortfolios is required for successful and effective implementation. Strategies and practical examples provide readers with a framework for undertaking this approach on their own campuses. In addition to the strategies and examples presented here, we have also developed a web companion to this book (http://documentinglearning.com). There you will be able to access additional ePortfolio examples, see the way that different tools are being used to implement ePortfolio projects on campuses, explore some of the campuses mentioned here in more detail, and link to the broader ePortfolio community.

We have written this book primarily with faculty instructors in mind. We therefore pay particular attention to the issues that they need to consider when planning for ePortfolio implementation. At the same time, we also address the issue of documenting learning from a stakeholder's approach—an approach that is iterative and practical in nature. We hope, however, that in considering the various perspectives a faculty instructor will keep in mind that the ideas presented here will also be useful to other campus partners who are exploring ePortfolios as a way for learners to document and make connections among their various learning experiences.

Acknowledgments

The field of ePortfolios, though growing, is still a fairly small circle of colleagues. As a group we share our experiences and care very much about supporting each other's efforts, mentoring those who become interested in the field, and being guided by those who have gone before us. So, in a sense, our appreciation goes to all who share our enthusiasm for ePortfolios, especially those students who have experimented with ePortfolios to document their learning and shared with us their transformative experiences of how they learn. We have showcased only a few of their experiences here but continue to draw inspiration from their ongoing efforts to change themselves and the world through the ideas and experiences captured in their ePortfolios.

We have also benefited greatly from being part of a community of researchers, teachers, and scholars of ePortfolios who have shared their enthusiasm and expertise with us. In particular, we would like to thank Helen Barrett; Trent Batson, Judy Williamson Batson, and Gary Brown of the Association for Authentic Experiential Evidence Based Learning (AAEEBL); Tom Carey, formerly of the University of Waterloo, for suggesting many years ago that ePortfolios might be an interesting approach to explore and who provided the latitude to do so; Bret Eynon, Randy Bass, and the entire Connect to Learning (C2L) Project team; Ali Jafari; Susan Kahn; Terrel Rhodes and Wende Garrison of the Association of American Colleges and Universities. We have all benefited greatly from participating in different cohorts of the Inter/National Coalition for Electronic Portfolio Research (I/NCEPR)—we thank all of our colleagues in those cohorts who shared their experiences and expertise with us. Of course, we could not have had those great experiences without the leadership of Darren Cambridge, Barbara Cambridge, and Kathleen Yancey. We have also benefited from working with many involved in the creation and support of various ePortfolio tools including Toru Iiyoshi of the KEEP Toolkit; Jeffrey Yan and Kelly Driscoll at Digication; Steve Adler and Molly Aiken at Adobe; and Webster Thompson at TaskStream.

In a very real sense the content of this book rests on the shoulders of those doing exciting and interesting work on their campuses who were willing to share both their successes and trials with us. We are grateful to all of them including: Evangeline Harris Stefanakis at Boston University; Giulia Guarnieri at Bronx Community College (CUNY); Sara E. Johnson and Norma Quirarte at California State University Fullerton; Gail Ring, Jennifer Johnson, Nathan Newsom, and David Pearson at Clemson University; Carmine Balascio and Kathleen Pusecker at the University of Delaware; Una Daly and Phyllis Spragge of Foothill Community College; Kristin Norris, Mary Price, and Kathryn Steinberg at Indiana University-Purdue University Indianapolis; Thomas Brumm of Iowa State University; James Griffin, Maureen Dumas, and Greg Lorenz at Johnson and Wales University; J. Elizabeth Clark of LaGuardia Community College; Joseph Ugoretz at William E. Macaulay Honors College (CUNY); Nancy Pawlyshyn at Mercy College; Kristina Hoeppner, Luke Baird, and Jon Bowen of MyPortfolio in New Zealand; Glenn Johnson at Penn State University; Jean Darcy at Queensborough Community College (CUNY); Kevin Kelly, Ruth Cox, Savita Malik, Oscar Macias, and Alycia Shada at San Francisco State University; Thomas Black, Reid Kallman, Celeste Fowles Nguyen, Sheri Sheppard, Robert Emery Smith, the Stanford d.school and the Office of the Vice Provost for Undergraduate Education at Stanford University; Nancy Wozniak and Sourav Tamang at SUNY Stony Brook; Toni Serafini, Carm De Santis, Vanessa LeBlond, Alex Romanowski, and Michelle Donaldson at St. Jerome's University; Laura Gambino at Tunxis Community College; Katherine Lithgow, Bob Sproule, and Chris Moffat at the University of Waterloo; Marc Zaldivar and Teggin Summers at Virginia Tech University; Diane L. Johnson, Janet W. Schnitz, Kyle Moreton, and Geri Nicastro at Western Governors University.

Taking on the writing of this book was both a labor of love and a challenge of great proportions. Choosing from the many amazing stories and pulling together a meaningful and useful document that we hope encourages colleagues to move from wherever they are in the process to the next step was the challenge we accepted. We hope we have succeeded. Of course, we could not have reached our goal without the generosity and assistance of so many. A special thanks go to our families who have given up numerous evenings, dinners, and even family vacations as we worked to finish this book: Thom, Emma, and Meghan Light and John, Elizabeth, and Lucy Higgins, as well as Mary Chen and Millicent Higgins. We especially thank Bobbi L. Kamil for providing wonderful support and for being a cheerleader and copyeditor. Finally, we thank our editor, Erin Null, for her wisdom, support, and feedback on the book.

About the Authors

Tracy Penny Light is an assistant professor at St. Jerome's University in the University of Waterloo in Ontario, Canada. Tracy's background in faculty development (she has designed and developed teaching and learning workshops on a variety of issues and codesigned the University of Waterloo's Teaching Excellence Academy for faculty) has served Tracy well in her own use of ePortfolios in the classroom since 2004. Prior to coming to St. Jerome's in 2007, she managed strategic learning projects for the associate vice president, Learning Resources and Innovation at the University of Waterloo, a position that included introducing ePortfolios to the campus in a number of programs, including Accounting and Financial Management, History, Co-operative Education, and Residence Life. Tracy's ongoing research focuses on ePortfolio implementation and the ability for reflection in ePortfolios to transform the student experience. Tracy also coauthored with Helen L. Chen the monograph *Electronic Portfolios and Student Success: Effectiveness, Efficiency, and Learning*, published by the Association of American Colleges and Universities in 2010, among other publications. She gives workshops and consults with campuses regularly (with Helen and John) on ePortfolio implementation. Tracy is also vice chair of the board of directors for the Association for Authentic, Experiential and Evidence-Based Learning (AAEEBL).

Helen L. Chen holds the position of research scientist, Department of Mechanical Engineering and is the project manager for ePortfolio Initiatives in the Office of the Registrar at Stanford University. Helen co-led the development of Folio Thinking, a reflective practice that situates and guides the effective use of learning portfolios through collaborations with national and international portfolio researchers. She is a founding member and cofacilitator of EPAC, a community of practice focusing on pedagogical and technological issues related to ePortfolios. Helen was a member of the National Advisory Board for the Valid Assessment of Learning in Undergraduate Education (VALUE) project led by the Association of American Colleges and Universities (AAC&U) and has served as a faculty member for their Institute on General Education and Assessment. She is also the director of research for the Association for Authentic, Experiential and Evidence-Based Learning (AAEEBL) and a senior scholar on LaGuardia Community College's Connect to Learning project, funded by FIPSE (Fund for the Improvement of Postsecondary Education). Helen's current research interests are focused in three areas: issues of academic and professional persistence in engineering education; documenting and measuring the impact of technology-augmented learning environments and active learning classrooms on innovations in teaching and learning; and the applications of Folio Thinking pedagogy and practices in general education, the disciplines, and in student affairs as facilitated by the use of ePortfolios and other web-based tools.

John Ittelson currently serves as director of outreach to the California Virtual Campus. John's primary interest is in ePortfolio development. John was involved from the beginning in the development of the California State University (CSU) CalState TEACH Program, and its evaluation. It is now a mainstay of CSU's electronic/mentoring teacher education efforts. He continues to consult to the project for California State University Monterey Bay (CSUMB). John has also been involved with CSU's NSF Noyces Scholars, helping develop better math and science skills for teaching math and science skills. John was a faculty member for thirty years, first at CSU Chico and then as a founding faculty member at CSUMB. During 2001–2002, John was selected to be one of two National Learning Infrastructure Initiative (NLII) EDUCAUSE Fellows. In that role he served as the lead for a conference focused on ePortfolios and held at Northwestern University. In 2003, he was named one of twenty-five California State University faculty members to receive the Bautzer University Faculty Advancement Award. Additionally, he sits on the boards of Access Monterey Peninsula Cable Consortium, the California Association for Supervision and Curriculum Development, Pacific Metrics, and the National Board of the Center for Interactive Learning and Collaboration (CLIC). John has been appointed as an Apple Distinguished Educator, an Adobe Educational Leader, and serves as a cofacilitator for the EPAC community of practice. He is also the cochair of the Academic ePortfolio Workgroup for Postsecondary Educational Standards Council (PESC).

Documenting Learning with ePortfolios

Introduction

The idea for this book grew out of our experiences running workshops and consulting with colleagues at university and college campuses in the United States and Canada who were interested in implementing ePortfolios. We were also inspired by collaborations with learners who have documented their learning in ePortfolios in our classrooms and programs. Since 2004 we have been refining our approach to documenting learning as we have worked with colleagues to design and implement their own ePortfolio initiatives. From that work, we were able to outline eight critical issues to consider for the effective and efficient implementation of ePortfolios (Chen and Penny Light, 2010). This book explores those issues in more detail by presenting a series of guiding questions within an ePortfolio implementation framework.

EPORTFOLIO IMPLEMENTATION FRAMEWORK

Table I.1 maps the eight critical issues for ePortfolios and student success identified by Chen and Penny Light (2010) to an ePortfolio implementation framework. The operationalization of these issues into specific tasks to take when planning and piloting an ePortfolio initiative describes and reinforces an iterative process that is not necessarily sequential nor successively developed; some of these tasks can run in parallel and may be revisited and revised more than once. For example, as an ePortfolio project evolves and begins to scale from the pilot stage, the learning outcomes may change and prioritization of stakeholders will shift.

Table I.1   ePortfolio Implementation Framework

Eight Critical Issues for ePortfolios and Student Success	The Framework: Steps and Guiding Questions
1. Defining learning outcomes	*Defining Learning Outcomes:* What are the learning outcomes for your ePortfolio initiative? What types of learning do you want to capture and document?
2. Understanding your learners 3. Identifying stakeholders	*Understanding Learners and Identifying Stakeholders:* Who are your stakeholders, especially your learners (the people who will be creating and using the ePortfolio)? How can they benefit from ePortfolios (i.e., what are their needs)? What can they contribute to and how can they support an ePortfolio effort?
4. Designing learning activities	*Designing Learning Activities:* Given your outcomes, what activities can you design to best guide the ways that learners use the ePortfolio to document their learning? How will their learning be captured and documented in the ePortfolio? How can the artifacts and evidence that are captured be organized, connected, and shared in meaningful and integrated ways?
5. Using rubrics to evaluate ePortfolios 6. Anticipating external uses of evidence	*Informing Assessment of Student Learning:* How do the ePortfolios and their artifacts inform assessment of student learning? In other words, what evidence results from how learners document their achievements and competencies? How can rubrics be used to support ePortfolio assessment?
7. Including multiple forms of evidence	*Using ePortfolio Tools and Technologies:* Which ePortfolio tools and technologies will allow you to collect the types of evidence that will allow learners to document and demonstrate their learning? What additional resources are needed (e.g., IT support) in order for your ePortfolio initiative to succeed?
8. Evaluating the impact of ePortfolios	*Evaluating The Impact of Your ePortfolio Initiative:* What kinds of evidence would validate the investment of time and resources to ePortfolios to all stakeholders? In other words, how might the documentation of learning collected in ePortfolios be used by other stakeholders on your campus (i.e., in accreditation efforts)? How will you evaluate whether or not your ePortfolio initiative was a success?

Additional factors to consider in the pre-planning stages of introducing ePortfolios include the *culture of the department, program, or institution* such as how knowledgeable faculty and students are about portfolio-related practices as well as their comfort level and experience with technology. Another factor is the *timeline for implementation,* which may relate to external pressures (e.g., where the institution is in its accreditation cycle or review of general education) or to internal constraints (e.g., the introduction of a new course or learning management system, a new provost or dean) that could motivate or incentivize the exploration of ePortfolios.

What the framework makes salient, we believe, is the need to think carefully about each of the issues through a series of prompting questions. This is not a hierarchical or step-by-step process. Rather, it is an iterative one, where the project leaders regularly review and revisit the learning goals of the ePortfolio implementation. Perhaps the most important need is that the purpose of the ePortfolio initiative be clear to the various stakeholders who have an interest in how student learning is documented. Over the years we have come to believe that this process of engaging the relevant stakeholders within a campus culture is critical in order for such an undertaking to be successful. As a result, you will find that considering the needs of the stakeholders on campus plays an integral role in each section of this book. Also central to our approach is the principle that the pedagogy MUST lead the technology. Although new technologies are often alluring for faculty instructors and students alike and are often what draws them to a particular approach, we know that without a clear pedagogical purpose, technology can be more show than substance. Instead, we advocate that clear learning outcomes be identified for an ePortfolio initiative and these outcomes need to be articulated in a way that is meaningful for all stakeholders involved with or affected by the implementation. Despite the fact that we end the book with a chapter on evaluating the impact of ePortfolios, we actually believe that it is important to always keep the overall goals in mind while thinking about how the initiative can be evaluated in terms of whether the goals were met and what evidence is available to demonstrate this has occurred. It is important to realize that this is not a step that occurs last, but rather throughout the implementation process. Those leading the ePortfolio implementation initiative ought to consider early and often how they will evaluate the success of the ePortfolio project, while always keeping in mind what changes need to be made in order to ensure that the goals or outcomes identified at the beginning of the project are being met during and at the end of the initiative.

As a way of framing this type of iterative thinking, we suggest starting with Richard L. Venezky's "history of the future" exercise (2001). The purpose of this exercise is to ensure that project goals are clearly stated and that the means by which the goals are achieved are articulated so that an evaluation plan can be developed (Chen and Penny Light, 2010). We have adapted this exercise in order to make it applicable and relevant to ePortfolios.

History of the Future Exercise

Imagine that your ePortfolio project is completed and that it succeeded in all of its goals. You are to appear tomorrow at a press conference to explain what you have accomplished. Write a press release to distribute at this meeting, explaining in a few paragraphs what it is that you have accomplished, who is benefiting from ePortfolios, why they are important tools for documenting learning (what problem does their use solve and why did it need to be solved in the first place?), and what it was that you did that led to or caused this success.

Source: Adapted from Venezky, 2001, p.18.

By completing this exercise at the beginning of a project and revisiting it periodically, you can clearly communicate the desired outcomes, why they are important, and how they can be achieved.

We believe that documenting learning is crucial for today's learners—not only to help them be successful in their personal and professional lives, but also to enhance their development as responsible citizens. We have an opportunity in higher education today to develop the kind of learners who have the power to transform our world—indeed, ePortfolios are transformative learning tools, not only for the learners and their instructors but also for a broader community of stakeholders. We hope that this book and its accompanying web site with additional resources and expanded examples at http://documentinglearning.com will provide you with some assistance to guide you in your exploration of the use of ePortfolios to document learning.

PART 1

Documenting Learning with ePortfolios

Part One discusses some of the theories that inform how ePortfolios can be used for documenting learning. We explore the reasons *why* instructors would implement ePortfolios and *how* documenting learning can assist learners to be more engaged and responsible citizens.

Why Document Learning?

earning today is a complicated business. New technologies are pushing the boundaries for learners as they seek to navigate a global world where information is quite literally at their fingertips. Yet, the way that learners *use* the information is often in question because they do not seem to be effectively analyzing the material that they find (Batson and Watson, 2011). More and more, instructors lament their students' lack of critical thinking abilities that will allow them to be successful learners and yet, increasingly, critical thinking is becoming a core competency for colleges and universities. Documenting learning is perhaps one of the most important ways for students to develop their critical thinking skills. Proponents of the ePortfolio movement have argued for well over a decade now that learners need to document what they know, reflect on their knowledge, and present that knowledge to specific audiences in order to learn deeply (Barrett, 2004, 2006; Cambridge, 2010). As many have pointed out, deep learning (Ramsden, 2003 Biggs, 1987; Biggs and Tang, 2007; Trigwell, Prosser, and Waterhouse, 1997; Kuh, et al., 2005), should be the goal of learners today and that learning should be lifelong. Ideally, students should internalize what they are learning because they are genuinely interested in the task, want to challenge themselves, and wish to increase their competence—that is, students should follow a mastery orientation to learning, rather than a performance goal orientation aimed at giving the teacher what they think he or she wants in order to get a good grade (Dweck, 1986; Ames and Archer, 1988). As Darren

Cambridge notes in his book, *Eportfolios for Lifelong Learning and Assessment*, "a major purpose of education is enabling individuals to have agency in the world through their evolving understanding of themselves, their capabilities, and their connections to others" (2010, ix). In other words, learners need to understand what they know and are able to do but, more important, *how* they know what they know in addition to what they do not know, as a way of strategizing where to learn next. Without this agency and ability to take control of their learning, students can "swirl" while in school and this can continue into their working life (Batson and Watson, 2011). Documenting learning in an ePortfolio, then, is a way for learners to explore and reflect on their knowledge by asking critical questions about where and how their knowledge was derived and what to learn next. As Cambridge puts it, "ePortfolios provide a lens for examining these questions and a means to put the answers into practice" (2010, ix). The process of reflecting on and questioning knowledge while thoughtfully articulating next steps is important for all types of learners whether they are individual student learners, faculty members, administrators, or even entire institutions.

The practice of documenting learning is not restricted to individuals; however, we focus in this book on student ePortfolios from the perspective of faculty instructors while also paying attention to the ways that student ePortfolios are valuable for different stakeholders, specifically, students themselves, faculty instructors, student affairs practitioners, and those interested in various types of assessment. Because ePortfolios enable learners to represent their own learning in a way that makes sense to them, they provide a window into the way that they have both *lived* and *experienced* different curricula—what Kathleen Yancey (1998) in Figure 1.1 refers to as the multiple curricula within higher education: the *delivered* curriculum, which is defined by the faculty and described in the syllabus; the *experienced* curriculum, which is represented by what is actually practiced by the student in the classroom; and the *lived* curriculum, which is based on the individual student's cumulative learning to date.

This chapter explores the ways in which learning can be (and should be) documented and how ePortfolios can be used for this purpose. *Folio thinking*, the reflective practice of creating ePortfolios (Chen and Mazow, 2002; Chen, Cannon, Gabrio, and Leifer, 2005; Chen, 2009), is central to this documentation and we pay particular attention to the rationale behind this process-oriented practice as it is connected to learners' abilities to develop the intellectual and social identities of

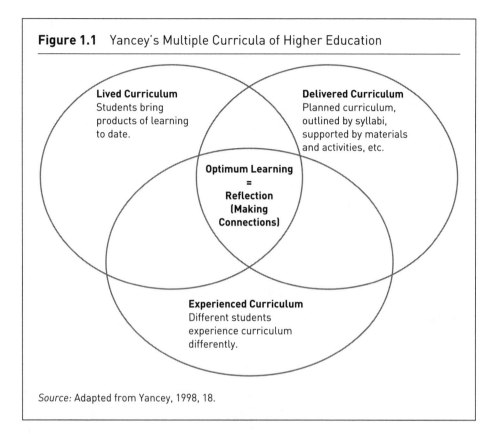

Figure 1.1 Yancey's Multiple Curricula of Higher Education

Lived Curriculum
Students bring products of learning to date.

Delivered Curriculum
Planned curriculum, outlined by syllabi, supported by materials and activities, etc.

Optimum Learning
=
Reflection
(Making Connections)

Experienced Curriculum
Different students experience curriculum differently.

Source: Adapted from Yancey, 1998, 18.

responsible and engaged citizens who are capable of complex decision making in a democratic society. We conclude the chapter by considering how documenting learning can also provide coherence for the work that students, faculty, student affairs, and assessment offices perform and how this can also inform the ways that evidence of learning from different contexts is collected via ePortfolios to support learning in an increasingly technological and globalized world.

FOLIO THINKING AND REFLECTION: THE KEY TO DOCUMENTING LEARNING

ePortfolios offer a framework within which students can personalize their learning experiences, and create different representations of their learning experiences tailored to specific audiences while also developing multimedia capabilities (Chen and Penny Light, 2010). Though the ePortfolio tool itself serves as a central place to capture the learning that happens in a variety of contexts (academic, workplace, and community) by collecting evidence from those contexts, making sense of that learning requires focused reflection on those experiences. Figure 1.2 illustrates the University of Waterloo's ePortfolio project, which emphasizes the need for integration of learning in different contexts. Students develop competency in the domain of their choice (i.e., their disciplinary major) while also reflecting on and integrating the learning that happens in academic, workplace, and community learning contexts).

Folio thinking is a reflective practice that situates and guides the effective use of learning portfolios. Drawing upon the literature in experiential learning, metacognition, reflective and critical thinking, mastery orientations to learning, and, of course, learning portfolios, folio thinking aims to encourage students to integrate

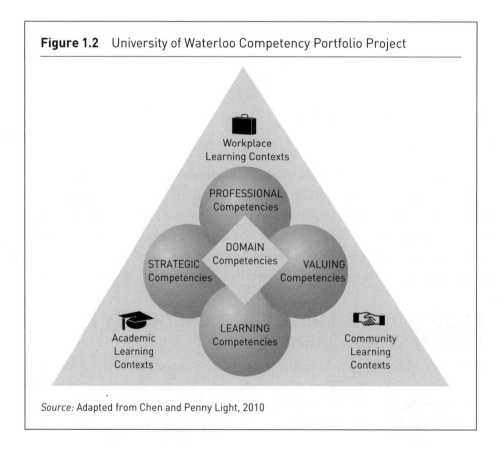

Figure 1.2   University of Waterloo Competency Portfolio Project

Source: Adapted from Chen and Penny Light, 2010

discrete learning experiences, enhance their self-understanding, promote taking responsibility for their own learning, and support them in developing an intellectual identity. (Chen and, 2002; Chen, Cannon, Gabrio, and Leifer, 2005; Chen, 2009).

Central to folio thinking and ePortfolios is the process of reflecting on the growth of one's knowledge and capabilities over time with an emphasis on metacognition (Brown, Peterson, Wilson, and Ptaszynski, 2008) by intentionally providing structured time and space for learners to consider and document the process of their learning and not just the product (assignments, tests, and so on). This process highlights the affordances of ePortfolios as not only potentially transformational with respect to individual learning and development but also the effectiveness of ePortfolios as assessment tools (Chen and Penny Light, 2010). Their use for both formative and summative assessment is seen in learners assessing their own knowledge. At the same time, others (instructors, employers, institutions) can use ePortfolios to assess the learners' skills and abilities for a variety of purposes, whether it is their ability to meet objectives in a course; to perform certain tasks, such as their suitability for a particular job; or to demonstrate institution-specific outcomes for accreditation. However, ePortfolios are much different from other assessment tools because they enable students to authentically represent their own learning in a way that makes sense to them and encourages them, ultimately, to take responsibility for their own learning.

Opportunities for Documenting Learning for Identity Development

The ability of learners to take responsibility for what they know through self-authorship is an important skill (Baxter Magolda, 2004; see Figure 1.3). In her work on learning partnerships and study of several national reports on higher education, Marcia Baxter Magolda asserts that a holistic approach to learning is required today in order to promote *intentional* learning, which allows for the integration of "cognitive, identity, and relationship dimensions of learning ... [to illustrate] the complexity of undergraduate learning required to address the complexity of contemporary campus and adult life" (2004, 5). In essence, students need to be able to understand where their knowledge comes from and how they have come to know what they know, but also to apply that knowledge in a changing world. She suggests that "the systemic thinking, the ability to judge knowledge claims offered by authorities, constructing convictions, and

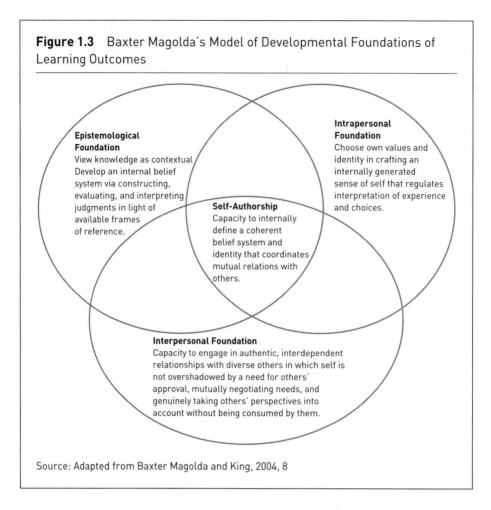

Figure 1.3 Baxter Magolda's Model of Developmental Foundations of Learning Outcomes

Epistemological Foundation
View knowledge as contextual Develop an internal belief system via constructing, evaluating, and interpreting judgments in light of available frames of reference.

Intrapersonal Foundation
Choose own values and identity in crafting an internally generated sense of self that regulates interpretation of experience and choices.

Self-Authorship
Capacity to internally define a coherent belief system and identity that coordinates mutual relations with others.

Interpersonal Foundation
Capacity to engage in authentic, interdependent relationships with diverse others in which self is not overshadowed by a need for others' approval, mutually negotiating needs, and genuinely taking others' perspectives into account without being consumed by them.

Source: Adapted from Baxter Magolda and King, 2004, 8

openness to new possibilities" are all part of what higher education is about. The ability of learners to be aware of their "own role in composing reality" (3) is important for their eventual role in the world. Ideally, learners should be able to engage with the world in a variety of ways as they develop an integrated sense of themselves through their interactions with the world. Of course, these abilities call into action a wide variety of skills ranging from critical thinking to more specific skills related to knowledge acquisition and construction. At the heart of the process, though, is reflection; Baxter-Magolda defines self-authorship as the "capacity to internally define a coherent belief system and identity that coordinates mutual relations with others" (8). This capacity is best developed through reflective (guided and unguided) practices that engage learners in the process of asking questions about what they know and how they know it in terms of their "epistemological," "intrapersonal," and "interpersonal" foundations; her argument forms the basis for developing "cognitive maturity, integrated identity, mature relationships, and effective citizenship" (8).

These different foundations for learning represent the knowledge development (both intellectual and social) that we advocate to achieve success in our world and which ePortfolios so richly enable. They provide structure for learners to manage the knowledge that they gain both inside and outside the classroom. Students today have access to more information than in the past. They have the ability to network with their friends and family members online, to make connections to a variety of contacts for both professional and personal reasons, and to tap into those networks for answers to thoughts or questions that they might have. The challenge that exists when learners have so much information at their fingertips is how to clearly organize, connect, and evaluate that information—how to become, as Baxter Magolda advocates, "self-authors." Beyond making connections *between* information, learners also need to *think through* how that information helps them to *know* and *understand* the world—in other words, to understand how their existing knowledge provides a framework for their understanding, how their values shape those frameworks, and how the relationships they engage in provide alternate perspectives (8).

In the example shown in Figure 1.4 and its accompanying text box (the first reflection written at the beginning of a course on sexual ethics), the student, Vanessa, clearly connects her existing knowledge about sexual ethics to her own values as well as to the relationship with her mother that provides a framework for her to understand the course material.

For educators, one of the challenges of dealing with today's learners is how to manage the existing knowledge and expectations that come into the classroom and that shape and frame the way that students understand material presented to them. Providing students with an opportunity to articulate why it is they know what they know is essential for learning and making connections. This example also highlights how useful it is for the instructor to have a clear sense of where students are coming from in order to move through the course materials in a way that will be meaningful for them.

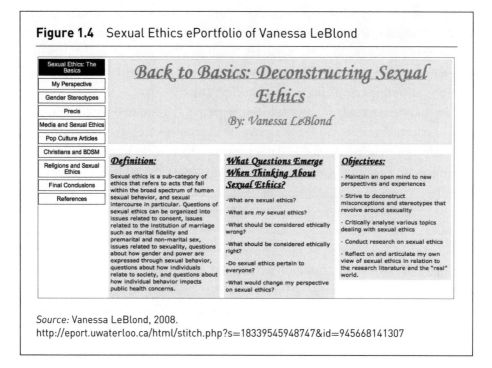

Figure 1.4 Sexual Ethics ePortfolio of Vanessa LeBlond

Source: Vanessa LeBlond, 2008.
http://eport.uwaterloo.ca/html/stitch.php?s=18339545948747&id=945668141307

"I think of myself as a very liberal and open-minded person, so my personal belief on the subject is that there shouldn't be such strict forms and restrictions in regards to sexuality, because it is fluid. I feel that people should be able to do what they want with whomever they choose, so long as they (and all people involved) are consenting, and not hurting anyone else (unless, of course, pain is part of what was consented to in some cases). I think I hold this view because of my own personality and experiences, but also in part because of how I was raised. I was raised in a Catholic family, but my mother has always been very liberal and talked to me openly about many subjects. Because of that, I have gained the view that people should be allowed to follow their own sexuality, because ethics implies that there are right and wrong ways of fulfilling your sexuality. I think in most cases, that isn't true."

Learning in this new paradigm, then, involves the ability of learners to integrate all of the information that they have with new information that they gain while at college or university. As Mary Taylor Huber and Pat Hutchings have pointed out, "one of the greatest challenges in higher education is to foster students' abilities to integrate their learning across contexts and over time. Learning that helps develop integrative capacities is important because it builds habits of mind that prepare students to make informed judgments in the conduct of personal, professional, and civic life" (2004, 1). In other words, integrative learning with ePortfolios encourages students to document their own educational journey over time and across the various domains of their lives as they demonstrate their skills and abilities.

The concept of the learning landscape (see Figure 1.5) acknowledges the learning that students engage in beyond the rigid structure of degree outcomes and requirements.

Experiences from a variety of learning contexts can be incorporated, including social networking with faculty mentors, peers, and employers. Most instructors design learning activities based on the ways that they were taught in their own disciplinary contexts. However, contemporary learners approach their understanding of particular materials in a very different way from the learners of even ten years ago. Today, it is not just a question of ensuring that students have learned the material in order to pass tests and exams, or even to move on to the next course. Rather, learners need to evaluate the knowledge claims offered by authorities, construct their own convictions, seek out new possibilities and sources, and apply the knowledge they are acquiring to complex real-world problems. As Baxter-Magolda and King (2004) point out, learners need to be aware of their own role in composing reality as they move through the world—they need to develop a sense of how and why they have particular belief systems, where those belief systems were developed, and what points in their learning caused their belief systems to shift or change. As Vanessa points out in her Sexual Ethics ePortfolio,

> Since the beginning of this semester, my view on sexual ethics has changed. In watching the movie *Kids* I realize even more how many people, and more importantly kids, are walking around without any sexual ethics. I think it is important for people to have respect for each other as sexual human beings and that consent and education are incredibly important.

This shift in Vanessa's thinking demonstrates the way that her reflection on new materials presented during the course facilitated her internalization of ideas that were meaningful for her. In this case, a film raised questions about the role of education in sexual ethics. This type of intellectual identity development is

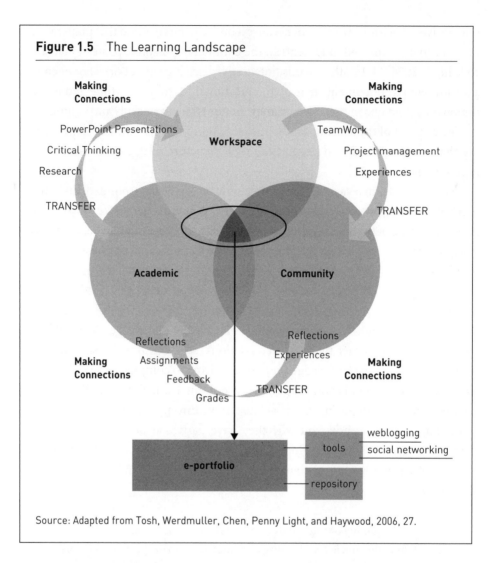

Figure 1.5 The Learning Landscape

Making Connections

Making Connections

PowerPoint Presentations

Critical Thinking

Research

TRANSFER

TeamWork

Project management

Experiences

TRANSFER

Workspace

Academic

Community

Reflections

Assignments

Feedback

Grades

Reflections

Experiences

TRANSFER

Making Connections

Making Connections

e-portfolio

tools

weblogging

social networking

repository

Source: Adapted from Tosh, Werdmuller, Chen, Penny Light, and Haywood, 2006, 27.

critical, of course, for students learning at college and university. Also important is the development of students' social identity, which is often found in how they represent themselves on social networking sites like Facebook, LinkedIn, or personal web sites (Williams, 2007). Ideally, learners should be encouraged to think through how those different identities are connected as Vanessa does in her ePortfolio. Facilitating these connections requires a more holistic approach to learning that emphasizes intentionality as a recurring theme and touchpoint in the process of identity development. In other words, the goal should be to foster learners' abilities to draw connections between their different identities and to be aware of when to take note of particular learning instances, gaps in their knowledge, and new strategies for moving forward. ePortfolios are useful for this type of learning because they allow learners to gather and store in one place the various artifacts that are evidence of their learning in different contexts.

This act of being able to represent one's own learning and, by connection, one's identity in relation to that learning is the most significant contribution of ePortfolios. Of course, at first, students do not always see the benefit of capturing their learning in an ePortfolio. Part of the requirements of using ePortfolios for learning is the need to clearly communicate to learners why they are using ePortfolios, how the use of ePortfolios will assist them in developing and documenting their own identities, and how that documentation can help them to make connections between the learning that happens in different contexts. We discuss the design of such learning instances more fully in Chapter Three, but it is important to note at this point the need for instructors to clearly communicate the goals and expectations of using ePortfolios in their classrooms.

Perhaps the most exciting part of exploring how ePortfolios can engage learners in developing their own identities is the transformative potential of such tools for allowing learners to reflect on who they are and how their knowledge, skills, and abilities will allow them to contribute to the world. While the value of this goal is widely acknowledged, in institutions of higher education we spend far too little time focusing on this important aspect of learning. Instead, we tend to emphasize the content to be learned and, by extrapolation, the products of that learning. However, as instructors we have a moral imperative to focus on the *process* of learning. This approach ensures that learners who graduate from our institutions develop the habits of mind in order to contribute meaningfully to society. A focus on student engagement or responsible citizenship is important to ensure that our learners are mindful about the fact that they will, indeed, need to contribute in some way to the world around them. Of course, this should not only happen in classrooms but should also form a significant part of what administrators, academic affairs, and student affairs leaders are doing to engage learners across institutions. The type of integrative learning by students that is captured in their ePortfolios is not only important for their own intellectual and social identity development, but the "containers" of authentic evidence that they create can also serve as a catalyst for conversations about what learning is occurring among faculty and other stakeholders within and across departments and programs (Chen and Penny Light, 2010). Mindful conversations among those who have a stake in students' documentation of their learning can help to create coherence across learning experiences and among stakeholders.

COHERENCE IN THE LEARNING EXPERIENCE

Students

Documenting learning for students is important for several reasons. First, students today need to be able to use technology mindfully and with a purpose. ePortfolios provide one way for students to engage with the online environment and social networking tools in an integrative way that promotes the development of their intellectual and social identities. With technological advances, students can document their learning using not only text reflections but also video blogs, audio recordings, and other media that demonstrate their knowledge, skills, and abilities to the world. ePortfolios provide a way for students to make a variety of connections as they develop both their social and intellectual capacities and skills (see Figure 1.6 for an example).

Faculty Instructors

Documenting learning for faculty is important in many respects. First, the ability to explore student ePortfolios provides instructors with easy access to formal and informal means of assessing the learning that is happening in their classrooms. Student reflections and other ePortfolio-related assignments offer instructors and students alike the opportunity to track learning over the course of the term. For instructors, this allows the timing and pace of course materials to be adjusted in the event that clarification is required of certain concepts or content, ensuring that student learning and engagement are maximized. For example, in the Sexual Ethics course mentioned earlier, many students, like Vanessa, indicated an interest in exploring in more detail the ways that sexual health education could have a positive impact on the development of sexual ethical behavior in young people. Because students provided that feedback while the course was still in progress, the instructor was able to make adjustments to the course topic schedule to facilitate this learning (an additional film was shown, a guest

Figure 1.6   History and Film ePortfolio of Chris Moffat

Introduction to ePortfolio

"History: More than Just Books" is the result of my experience in Dr. Penny-Light's HIST 200: History and Film course. It will portray the development of my ability to "do history" by showing how I have used critical thinking and the historical lens to interpret the past. The focus of the ePortfolio is my idea of a "Holistic Approach" to the study of history. The use of film as a primary source was emphasized in HIST 200, and I believe that this ideal can be spread into other aspects of art, particularly in the visual realm, music, and literature.

THE HOLISTIC APPROACH

Utilising Alternative Media:

Andrew Hunt's lecture on the Cold War was important in that it reflected the need for understanding context while 'doing history'. One can not even hope to understand how monumental events like the Cuban Missile Crisis were without understanding the climate of fear, tension and paranoia that gripped America from the end of the Second World

The Evolution of Critical Thinking in HIST 200

History and Film - Learning to "do history" by using more than just books , understanding the importance of context and the necessity for interpretation. These reflections chart my development in the course, my movement from a student with complete faith in books to an open-minded historian willing to escape the labyrinth of the library and experience the past through other sources.

Initial Reflection:
Through the Lens - A New View of History

Source: Chris Moffat, 2006 http://www.cfkeep.org/html/snapshot.php?id=89087256313383

speaker was brought in, and an online discussion was established). Beyond their formative assessment capabilities, student ePortfolios can also represent an excellent source for summative assessment. Faculty members can observe the learning that happens over the course of the term and ensure that learners have understood both the content and the process thinking specific to that discipline. Tools like rubrics are one way that faculty can assess student ePortfolios. Beyond the classroom, ePortfolios can also provide a window for others (chairs, deans, alumni, employers, and so on) to view what is happening within the classroom and on the campus. The learning that is occurring within a given course often goes unnoticed beyond the classroom; in other words, what happens in an individual faculty member's classroom often stays in the classroom. In addition, an ePortfolio component that is incorporated into multiple courses within a curriculum or department allows faculty members to not only observe how learning outcomes are being addressed and interpreted by students but also identify when concepts and content should be introduced and reinforced. This can help a department to ensure that students are actually achieving the learning that is required of graduates of a particular program. For example, in the Sexuality, Marriage, and Family Studies program in which the sexual ethics course mentioned earlier is located, department members identified milestones in the program where ethics could be developed and documented by students as they worked toward a capstone experience at the end of their degree (see Figure 1.7). This scaffolding of student learning will be discussed in further detail in Chapter Three.

Student Affairs and Beyond

There are many reasons why student ePortfolios can be useful to student affairs practitioners. In an age when student cocurricular learning is increasingly viewed as important as curricular learning, ePortfolios can provide a way for student affairs practitioners and faculty members to have a conversation about the ways in which those curricular and cocurricular learning outcomes are connected (Garis and Dalton, 2007). For instance, being aware of the various initiatives taking place on the student affairs side can help faculty members to think through the different

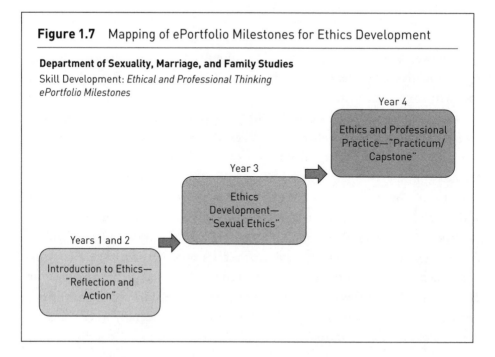

Figure 1.7   Mapping of ePortfolio Milestones for Ethics Development

Department of Sexuality, Marriage, and Family Studies
Skill Development: *Ethical and Professional Thinking*
ePortfolio Milestones

Year 4

Ethics and Professional Practice—"Practicum/ Capstone"

Year 3

Ethics Development— "Sexual Ethics"

Years 1 and 2

Introduction to Ethics— "Reflection and Action"

ways in which learning outcomes can be met and to facilitate knowledge transfer and deep learning among their students. For instance, in the sexual ethics course, students are encouraged to bring their work and volunteer experiences into their thinking about ethics. Because many students who take this course volunteer at agencies that provide sexual health education, they have an opportunity to integrate the learning that happens in that context with the theory and discussions presented in class. Similarly, in a history course where students are asked to develop their critical thinking skills or their historical thinking, students can provide evidence of how they do this in the history class and of the ways that they can apply similar kinds of thinking in other contexts. For example, an engineering student who is taking a history course can discuss how he engages in critical thinking in his history course, in his engineering classes, and while building a solar car for competition. Just as instructors can benefit from hearing about what types of learning is happening outside the classroom and better engage students, so too can other stakeholders on a campus. A living-learning program in residential life can contribute to the development of professional abilities such as teamwork skills in partnership with instructors who are teaching in the accounting program. This collaboration can provide extra opportunities for students to be introduced to such skills that can then be reinforced and mastered in residences where students have opportunities to build on the collaborative skills they have begun to develop in academic courses. Beyond student affairs practitioners, other stakeholders can be engaged in benefiting from the learning that is being documented in ePortfolios. For instance, alumni relations might gain insight into the kinds of activities and programs that are important and exciting for future alumni in order to establish a foundation for alumni relations after graduation.

Assessment

As mentioned earlier, assessment is an important aspect for all postsecondary institutions. Whether the purpose of the assessment is for accreditation or achievement of student learning outcomes, carefully designed assignments that incorporate an ePortfolio approach can result in a multimedia collection of evidence that is more authentic and more efficiently collected through partner-ships with students over time. Triangulation of both qualitative and quantitative data from student ePortfolios and sources like the National Survey of Student

Engagement (NSSE) program identifies ways in which students are meeting learning outcomes and can provide a more meaningful picture about the learning and engagement that is taking place on a particular campus (Eynon, 2009a).

DOCUMENTING LEARNING—INTEGRATED INSTRUCTION WITH BENEFITS FOR ALL

Regardless of which stakeholder group is using the ePortfolio, these tools provide a much richer set of data than traditional tools. An important task for faculty instructors using ePortfolios is thinking through which other stakeholders on their campus would be interested in the data contained within student ePortfolios. Although making a connection to student affairs practitioners may not be the focus of the ePortfolio initiative as a whole, being mindful of the variety of ways that the evidence in students' ePortfolios can be used by different stakeholders can assist faculty in developing uses for the ePortfolio beyond the classroom. In addition, an emphasis on the importance of documenting learning for students will communicate the importance and value of a more holistic approach to learning that is needed today. As a recent report released by AAC&U's National Council on Liberal Engagement and America's Promise (LEAP) indicates,

> Only a few years ago, Americans envisioned a future in which this nation would be the world's only superpower. Today, it is clear that the United States—and individual Americans—will be challenged to engage in unprecedented ways with the global community, collaboratively and competitively. These seismic waves of dislocating change will only intensify. The world in which today's students will make choices and compose lives is one of disruption rather than certainty, and of interdependence rather than insularity... The LEAP National Leadership Council recommends, in sum, an education that intentionally fosters, across multiple fields of study, wide-ranging knowledge of science, cultures, and society; high-level intellectual and practical skills; an active commitment to personal and social responsibility; and the demonstrated ability to apply learning to complex problems and challenges. The council further calls on educators to help students become "intentional learners" who focus, across ascending levels of study and diverse academic programs, on achieving the essential learning outcomes. But to help students do this, educational communities will also have to become

far more intentional themselves—both about the kinds of learning students need, and about effective educational practices that help students learn to integrate and apply their learning. (National Leadership Council for Liberal Education and America's Promise, 2007, 6–9)

The ability to document learning in ePortfolios affords the broader educational community within higher education with a potentially richer set of tools and practices to address the needs of not only today's learners but also the complex problems faced by our ever-changing society.

LEAP Essential Learning Outcomes

Beginning in school, and continuing at successively higher levels across their college studies, students should prepare for twenty-first-century challenges by gaining:

Knowledge of Human Cultures and the Physical and Natural World
- Through study in the sciences and mathematics, social sciences, humanities, histories, languages, and the arts

Focused by engagement with big questions, both contemporary and enduring

Intellectual and Practical Skills, including
- Inquiry and analysis
- Critical and creative thinking
- Written and oral communication
- Quantitative literacy
- Information literacy
- Teamwork and problem solving

Practiced extensively, across the curriculum, in the context of progressively more challenging problems, projects, and standards for performance

Personal and Social Responsibility, including
- Civic knowledge and engagement—local and global
- Intercultural knowledge and competence
- Ethical reasoning and action
- Foundations and skills for lifelong learning

Anchored through active involvement with diverse communities and real-world challenges

Integrative and Applied Learning, including

- Synthesis and advanced accomplishment across general and specialized studies

Demonstrated through the application of knowledge, skills, and responsibilities to new settings and complex problems

Note: This listing was developed through a multiyear dialogue with hundreds of colleges and universities about needed goals for student learning; analysis of a long series of recommendations and reports from the business community; and analysis of the accreditation requirements for engineering, business, nursing, and teacher education. The findings are documented in previous publications of the Association of American Colleges and Universities: *Greater Expectations: A New Vision for Learning as a Nation Goes to College* (2002), *Taking Responsibility for the Quality of the Baccalaureate Degree* (2004), and *College Learning for the New Global Century* (2007). For further information, see www.aacu.org/leap.

Source: Adapted from AAC&U, 2007. http://www.aacu.org/leap/documents/EssentialOutcomes_Chart .pdf.

A Stakeholder's Approach to Documenting Learning

One of the main goals of ePortfolio work is to develop students who are intentional and integrative learners. Chen and Penny Light (2010) outline eight critical implementation issues for individuals and campuses to consider as they plan for the use of ePortfolios to enhance student learning. The issues addressed in this approach include:

1. Defining learning outcomes
2. Understanding your learners
3. Identifying stakeholders
4. Designing learning activities
5. Including multiple forms of evidence
6. Using rubrics to evaluate ePortfolios
7. Anticipating external uses of evidence
8. Evaluating the impact of ePortfolios

As noted in the introduction, we have further operationalized these issues into a more succinct, iterative cycle within an ePortfolio Implementation Framework that focuses specifically on:

1. Defining learning outcomes
2. Identifying and understanding learners and stakeholders

3. Designing learning activities

4. Informing assessment of student learning

5. Using ePortfolio tools and technologies

6. Evaluating the impact of your ePortfolio initiative

More detail on each of these areas will be provided in the other chapters in this book.

While each of the original eight issues has its own strengths and related concerns, the concept of the "audience" (issue 3) is embedded throughout the implementation framework. We have learned through our discussions with various campuses that in order to create effective and efficient ePortfolio programs to support integrative learning, greater engagement with the various stakeholders who have something to gain from and contribute to the effort is critical. By extending this "stakeholder approach" more broadly across the framework and aligning these issues to specific stakeholder interests, we can more clearly define and tailor specific strategies for the design of an ePortfolio activity or program. This chapter outlines this approach by identifying ways to define stakeholders in a given context and then working through each of the steps in the framework. We also incorporate design principles from the Hasso Plattner Institute of Design at Stanford University (also known as the "d.school") to illuminate these different activities. For faculty instructors, this approach demonstrates that even efforts on a small, course-based scale can benefit from thinking more broadly about the stakeholder perspective.

IDENTIFYING INTEREST: SETTING THE PARAMETERS FOR A DEFINITION OF STAKEHOLDERS

The primary focus for any ePortfolio project is on how students can use the tool to document their learning across the various domains of their educational experiences, inside and outside the classroom, and over time. The constellation of stakeholders who might have an interest in reading, reviewing, and evaluating what is in the student ePortfolio is potentially wide and varied, as shown in Figure 2.1.

Although each of these stakeholders has the potential to benefit from and contribute to the ePortfolio initiative (Reese and Levy, 2009), the emphasis on documentation of learning leads to a focus on the stakeholders with interests

Figure 2.1 Constellation of Possible ePortfolio Stakeholders

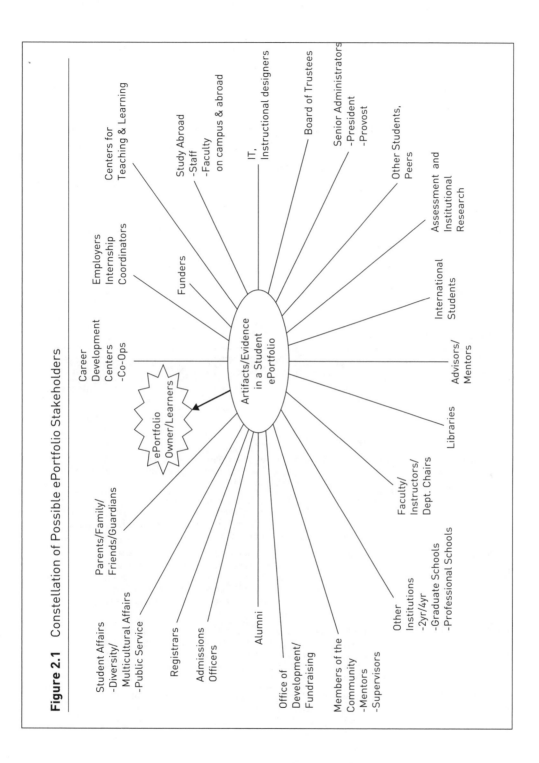

that directly map to faculty interests in ePortfolios. The aim of this approach is to capture varied aspects of student learning. Table 2.1 is a description of several stakeholder perspectives and a brief characterization of their unique view of ePortfolios.

For this chapter, the unique views of ePortfolios held by different stakeholders are explored in the context of the ways that faculty instructors facilitate the development of student ePortfolios at the course level, department or program level, and school or institutional level. The focus on these levels is based on where ePortfolios are most commonly introduced and piloted. An individual faculty member is often able to experiment with a new technology in a time-constrained fashion (such as in an individual course) and with limited resources, particularly with software that is readily available for free or at a minimal cost, such as web-based tools. As a "proof of concept," this kind of ePortfolio prototype primarily

Table 2.1 Description of ePortfolio Stakeholders

Stakeholder	Perspective
Students	As the owners and creators of the content of the ePortfolio, students are the most critical stakeholders in any ePortfolio initiative.
Faculty	Faculty, as the creators of the curriculum and the designers of the ePortfolio experience, define and establish the expectations and the culture of ePortfolio practice.
Academic Leaders	Academic leaders, including department chairs and deans, provide leadership and support for the ePortfolio project but also have their own stakeholders to whom they answer.
Administrators	Similar to academic leaders, presidents, provosts, and other key administrators will have varying interests in the kinds of evidence that ePortfolios can produce to inform, for example, accreditation efforts, institutional research, and external funders and boards of trustees.
Student Affairs	Career development centers, public and community service organizations, residential education, advising and mentoring services, and other extracurricular and cocurricular organizations share a more holistic view of students beyond the confines of the classroom. As a division, student affairs experts can be great partners and resources in any ePortfolio initiative.
Staff	Faculty developers, academic technologists, instructional designers, library staff, and campus registrars have valuable knowledge and experience to contribute to training, support, logistics, and long term vision of how ePortfolios can be integrated, scaled, and sustained within the university environment.
Assessment Experts	Assessment experts who are involved in department and program reviews, institutional research, and committees preparing for accreditation or external credentialing can also play a key role.

relies on the enthusiasm of an individual faculty member and can serve as a tangible example and case study for future discussions with other instructors, department chairs, and deans. Yet, the interests of other stakeholders are often not considered because of the need to think through the course-specific details. At times, instructors can feel isolated if they are the only innovator or "early adopter" on the campus. Engaging other stakeholders, at least in conversations about how ePortfolios can be useful to them, can be one way to build community around the development of this approach for documenting learning. In addition, through e-mail, listservs, web sites, and social networking tools, faculty members can tap into an international community of practitioners and like-minded instructors, researchers, administrators, and students who can serve as resources and colleagues. Taking a stakeholder approach can also facilitate these connections.

STANFORD "D.SCHOOL"

Although the emphasis of this book does not include the entire constellation of ePortfolio stakeholders, it does describe a process for gaining a more comprehensive understanding of any individual stakeholder in an ePortfolio initiative. This process is largely informed by the methods of "design thinking" promoted by the Stanford d.school. Design thinking draws upon interdisciplinary and cross-disciplinary approaches from design and engineering, business, arts, and social sciences through a "learning by doing" immersive experience of creative problem solving. The emphasis is always on an iterative process in which the process and not the outcome is most important. The d.school has developed a set of mindsets to consider while working through the design process (see Figure 2.2). Central to these are the need to have empathy for the people that the design is for, the willingness to develop prototypes that can be used to communicate the vision of the project, a collaborative approach, and the willingness to seek out and receive feedback throughout the process in each step. There is no "right" or "wrong" way to engage in this process—rather, designers (in this case, faculty instructors creating ePortfolio learning experiences) can approach their project from any of the mindsets with the goal of keeping the perspective of others in view. In other words, one could start with prototyping ("Embrace Experimentation" and "Show Don't Tell") and then mindfully move to another step (i.e., "Craft Clarity") in

Figure 2.2 D.Mindsets

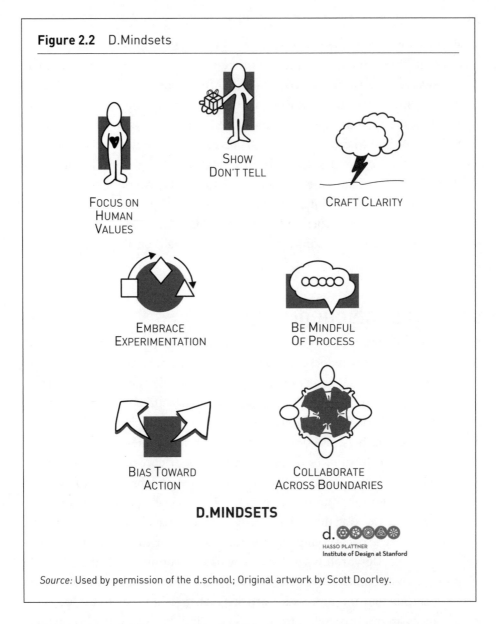

FOCUS ON
HUMAN
VALUES

SHOW
DON'T TELL

CRAFT CLARITY

EMBRACE
EXPERIMENTATION

BE MINDFUL
OF PROCESS

BIAS TOWARD
ACTION

COLLABORATE
ACROSS BOUNDARIES

D.MINDSETS

d.
HASSO PLATTNER
Institute of Design at Stanford

Source: Used by permission of the d.school; Original artwork by Scott Doorley.

order to communicate the vision for the project. Critical to any design project is the need to develop a plan for the outcomes that are desired. Without the outcomes clearly articulated, it is easy to lose sight of the end goal that you want to achieve. In the next section, several of the d.school principles are applied to our framework for ePortfolio implementation as guiding principles for the exploration of the stakeholder perspective (Hasso Plattner Institute of Design at Stanford, 2011).

D.Mindset: Craft Clarity

- *Produce a coherent vision out of messy problems. Frame it in a way to inspire others and to fuel ideation.*
  - Relevant ePortfolio Framework Step: Defining learning outcomes

A critical step in every ePortfolio project is to define the learning goals and outcomes for the initiative. Whether this begins at the institutional level or at the individual course level, this vision can be operationalized into actionable steps, activities, and tasks for specific stakeholder groups. The way in which this vision is framed should be tailored to the needs and interests of the specific stakeholder group(s) being addressed. For example, one d.school method is the "Point-of-View Want Ad" approach where the needs of the user and the designer's insights into user characteristics are embedded within the format of a want ad. This method can help identify a specific character trait or aspect of the problem through a more playful format. For example:

> **Undecided first year student seeks a tool to help me identify my academic passion(s). ABOUT ME**: I am not sure what I want to do with my life, interested in a range of majors (from religious studies to engineering), having a lot of fun at college but parents are pressuring me to declare a "practical" major. **YOU**: easily capture my thoughts through typing, audio, and video, remind me to think about my interests by asking me questions throughout the semester, help me view and organize my experiences visually, chronologically, and by related themes so I can see the big picture of what I'm actually doing, share my reflections and interests with my faculty, advisor, family, and friends. Mobile phone accessibility is a MUST!

This want ad highlights several user characteristics important in the design of an ePortfolio project. Through the development of this want ad, it becomes clear that this user would want to engage with an ePortfolio system that allowed them to document their learning in a variety of formats; for instance, the user indicates that a means to represent learning in a "visual" way is important. He or she also indicates a desire to make connections among learning experiences both chronologically and thematically, which might prompt the designer of this project to incorporate some kind of concept mapping activity or tagging feature within the ePortfolio itself, or in the course in which it is being used.

D.Mindset: Embrace Experimentation

- *Prototyping is not simply a way to validate an idea, it is an integral part of the innovation process. "We build to think and learn."*
  - Relevant ePortfolio Implementation Step: Designing learning activities

Designing reflective prompts, curriculum, and other ePortfolio-related tasks are both a challenge and an opportunity for creativity and innovation via an iterative prototyping cycle. Because the ePortfolio is electronic, the instinct is often to prototype online. However, prototyping in more concrete and tangible media using crayons and paper, Lego blocks, foam core, or clay can result in experiences and products that users can react to. Creating multiple concrete prototypes can result in new insights and unexpected realizations by creating a conversation between the designer and the design medium (Hartmann et al., 2006). At the same time, these simple prototypes are much easier to discard. Most designers find that once they put something into an electronic medium, even one as simple and low-stakes as PowerPoint, it is difficult to let go of them when feedback is received because these electronic prototypes look and feel more "finished." In addition, test users are often reluctant to be highly critical of such prototypes for the same reasons. By keeping prototypes simple, the goal of creating a sense of the project without constraining feedback can be achieved.

A simple activity might be to ask potential users to sketch what might go into an ePortfolio. This can be done in a couple of minutes by asking participants to put pen to paper to illustrate how they define an ePortfolio and what it might include (see Figure 2.3). These drawings of the artifacts they expect to see may reveal a great deal about who they are and what aspects of learning they think would be important to capture in an ePortfolio.

D.Mindset: Focus on Human Values

- *Empathy for the people for whom the ePortfolio is being designed; feedback from these users is fundamental to good design.*
  - Relevant ePortfolio Implementation Step: Identifying and understanding learners and stakeholders

Figure 2.3 Pen and Paper Sketch of What Kinds of Artifacts Might Go into an ePortfolio

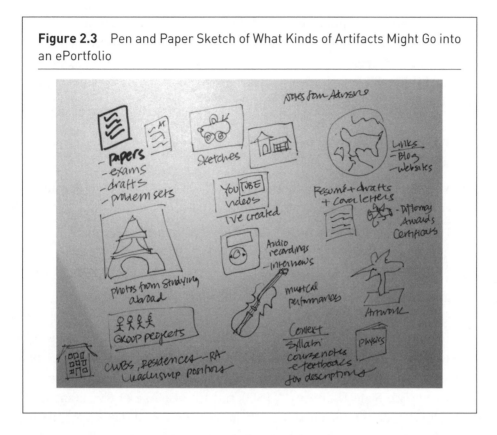

The d.school mindset of *empathy* helps to gain a deeper understanding of who the learners and stakeholders are and how the design of an ePortfolio and folio thinking culture (see Chapter One) can specifically address their needs and concerns. Using an "interview for empathy" approach enhances insight into the thoughts, emotions, and motivations of both learners and other stakeholders so that the designer can develop an innovative ePortfolio to meet their needs.

The interview method can be used in a variety of contexts. For example, in a workshop, participants can join in an exercise where they are paired up with a partner. In this setting, each partner interviews the other to elicit the attributes of one learner or stakeholder for their ePortfolio initiative. This approach can also be used on campuses where ePortfolio projects are just beginning or currently under way. In this scenario, a member of the ePortfolio leadership team conducts a series of interviews with identified stakeholders in order to learn more about their needs and desires for an ePortfolio. In both of these contexts, the aim is to ask questions that encourage the telling of stories from which it is possible to gain insights into how the learner or stakeholder thinks about the world. Some examples of possible questions might include:

- Who is the most critical stakeholder for your project? Who is the learner who will create or use an ePortfolio?

- Why does your learner or stakeholder NEED an ePortfolio? How do you envision him or her using the ePortfolio?

- How will your learner or stakeholder BENEFIT from the ePortfolio initiative or project?

- What can the learner or stakeholder CONTRIBUTE to the ePortfolio initiative or project?

It may also be useful to create a simple table to track the findings from your interviews as Reese and Levy (2009) have proposed. In Table 2.2, an excerpt from a report analyzing the use of ePortfolios in the Metro Academies Program at San Francisco State University (SFSU) and City College of San Francisco, Shada (2011) addresses the questions: *"Who are the potential stakeholders, what are the benefits, and what contributions can they make to help with a successful implementation?"* (21)

D.Mindset: Radical Collaboration

- *Bringing together innovators with varied backgrounds and viewpoints. Enables breakthrough insights and solutions to emerge from the diversity.*
  - Relevant ePortfolio Implementation Step: Identifying and understanding learners and stakeholders

The mindset of *radical collaboration* builds upon the knowledge that has been gained about the needs and concerns of the learners or stakeholders. Considering the constellation of stakeholders who are represented in Figure 2.1 and the diversity of perspectives and experiences of those individuals, there is clearly an opportunity within the ePortfolio community to engage these

Table 2.2 Potential Benefits and Contributions for ePortfolio Stakeholders in the Metro Academies Program at San Francisco State University (SFSU)

Stakeholder	Potential Benefits	Potential Contributions
Metro Funders	See clear examples of the work that the students accomplish in Metro, how they develop throughout the program, and what their money goes toward	Provide new or continued financial support for Metro and/or specifically for efforts around ePortfolios
SFSU Admissions Office	See a more comprehensive picture of student applicants	Begin to look at ePortfolios as part of an admissions packet
Metro Project Leadership	Assess program comprehensively; serves as a tool to help recruit funding and political support for the Metro program. Can help maintain relationships with alumni.	Support the ePortfolio program with funding allocation and administrative support (including support staff)

stakeholders as partners in the design of any ePortfolio effort. Insights, as well as resources, can come from unexpected places; reaching out to potential collaborators early on in the design process can result in a stronger network and a more sustainable ePortfolio initiative. Of course, for faculty instructors, the first group of stakeholders that should be considered are the learners themselves. Each institutional culture attracts and fosters learners of a particular type. It is always important for faculty members who are considering any classroom innovation to collect information about who those learners are—often, they are not necessarily who we think they are. Beyond collecting data that can be helpful in the design of an ePortfolio initiative, learners are more likely to be engaged in documenting their learning if they have played a role in the design and development of the approach.

D.Mindset: Show Don't Tell

- *Communicate the vision in an impactful and meaningful way by creating experiences using illustrative visuals and telling good stories.*
  - Relevant ePortfolio Implementation Step: Informing assessment of student learning (through evidence)

There are at least two related approaches to this concept of "vision." On the one hand, there is the vision for the ePortfolio initiative and how you, as the leader of the project, communicate this vision to various stakeholders in order to foster buy-in and interest in supporting this work. Equally important is your understanding of the motivations and needs of the stakeholders and the project leaders' ability to identify, collect, and present evidence and stories that are persuasive and compelling to the specific stakeholder being addressed.

With respect to defining a vision for your ePortfolio project, Figure 2.4 is one example that characterizes the academic trajectory or "learning career" of an undergraduate student and the experiences that he or she encounters both inside and outside of the classroom. This mapping emphasizes the student-centered nature of ePortfolios and how a culture of folio thinking can evolve over time. As a conversation starter, this approach has been useful in identifying the milestones where students may already be reflecting on and documenting their experiences. This type of map also helps stakeholders to understand their role in helping to guide and support students during their journey.

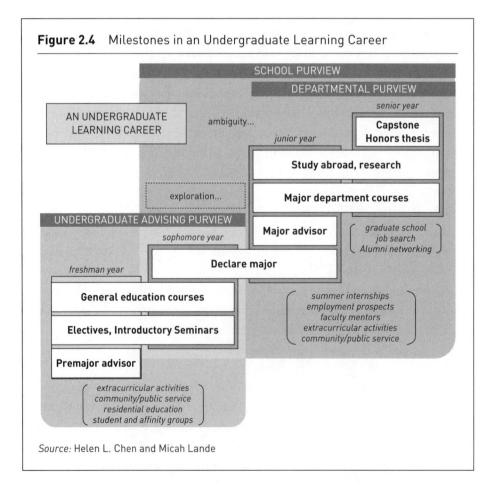

Figure 2.4 Milestones in an Undergraduate Learning Career

Source: Helen L. Chen and Micah Lande

Beyond providing stakeholders with a sense of when they might support learners in their documentation efforts, this map also identifies the points in a learning career where evidence of learning is collected that might be useful to different stakeholders. By communicating this pathway to multiple stakeholders, project leaders can initiate conversations about the amount and types of evidence that would be useful to stakeholders on the campus. This allows project leaders to ensure that opportunities for documentation and evidence gathering are not lost.

As noted earlier, the learning career offers many opportunities to collect evidence of student learning. The second aspect of this perspective focuses on the strategies that might be employed to communicate a vision that is supported by evidence and tailored to the specific stakeholder you are approaching. Much of this is derived from personal knowledge and understanding of the motivations and needs of the stakeholder obtained through interviews, stories, and observations using the process of collaboration mentioned earlier. It is critical to ensure that the evidence of learning collected at each stage of the learning career is meaningful to the stakeholder you are trying to engage. For some stakeholders, such as administrators, statistics about the number of institutions that are considering adopting ePortfolios or evidence of what peer institutions are doing might be persuasive. For chairs and deans, quantitative data from formal research studies showing that institutions with students who participated in courses with an ePortfolio component achieved greater student engagement and critical thinking—as has been demonstrated at LaGuardia Community College—might be of interest (Eynon, 2009a, 2009b). LaGuardia and Kapi'olani Community College (Eynon, 2009b and Kirkpatrick et al., 2009 as described in Cambridge, Cambridge, and Yancey, 2009) have gone on to correlate such evidence with other measures such as the Community College Survey of Student Engagement (CCSSE) and the Learning and Study Strategies Inventory (LASSI). Of course, in many instances, the qualitative evidence derived from student voices articulating the benefits of a folio thinking process from an introductory mechanical engineering seminar at Stanford University might also be compelling (Chen, Cannon, Gabrio, and Leifer, 2005):

> I'm planning to use the takeaway of reflective thinking intensely for my college years, and beyond. While I've been aware of my education before,

I think it's truly the mark of a higher education that the student takes responsibility for what they are learning, and is fully aware of the value of their time.

Given the multimedia nature of ePortfolios, this evidence could be represented by the curated collections of specific examples of student work that have been documented in ePortfolios—papers, sketches, audio recordings, photos, and videos—together with reflections that represent the student's perspective on his or her education.

D. Mindset: Be Mindful of Process

- *It is important to know where you are in the design process, what methods to use in that stage, and what your goals are.*
  - Relevant ePortfolio Implementation Step: Evaluating the impact of ePortfolios

As an ePortfolio initiative progresses, it is expected that the project stakeholders will evolve and change depending on what stage the project is in. For example, in the early stages of piloting and experimentation with the concept of an ePortfolio on a campus, the focus may be on working with individual faculty members to incorporate an ePortfolio component into their course curriculum. As interest in ePortfolios grows, you may build upon the pilots and begin to scale your efforts to address the specific concerns of department chairs and senior administrators as well as external funders.

In thinking about the process and the evolution of an ePortfolio initiative, it is important to begin to design the evaluation of the project concurrently as each phase of the project evolves.

The design of a plan to evaluate the impact of ePortfolios parallels the design of assessments of how student learning outcomes are achieved within an ePortfolio project. In Chapter Nine we will go into greater detail with an exercise to help clarify and articulate what the specific goals and project outcomes are, the methods by which they can be achieved, and the kinds of evidence that will demonstrate success and return on investment to the various stakeholders.

D.Mindset: Bias Toward Action

- *Design thinking is a misnomer. It is more about doing than thinking. Bias toward doing and making, over thinking and meeting.*
  - Relevant ePortfolio Implementation Step: Using ePortfolio tools and technologies

The digital, web-based, in the "cloud" nature of ePortfolios calls to mind an image of an individual communicating and interacting with the rest of the world through a screen, whether the screen is on a laptop computer or a mobile device. While acknowledging the importance of the ePortfolio technology and its advantages, the focus has been and will continue to be on building a culture of folio thinking and prioritizing the ePortfolio process and practice over ePortfolio technology. For example, in premajor advising at Stanford University (Chen and Black, 2010), the ePortfolio is intended to enhance the face-to-face interactions students have with their academic advisors through the folio thinking process by: (1) asking student advisees to update their ePortfolio (often guided by prompting questions) prior to meeting with their advisors, thereby emphasizing student responsibility to ensure the meeting is more productive and focused; and (2) referencing the ePortfolio artifacts during the advising meeting as a springboard for concrete discussion, asking questions about student work, and documenting feedback and action items. In this scenario, there is greater action on the part of both the advisor and the student, which hopefully will result in increased engagement as well as accountability. It is essential to interpret and apply the *bias towards action* mindset to how ePortfolios can enhance, expand, and expose students to relationships and opportunities that ultimately lead to face-to-face connections and interactions.

Stakeholders have a variety of needs that can potentially be addressed with ePortfolios. Understanding who the various stakeholders on a campus are and how ePortfolios might help meet their needs are essential elements of any ePortfolio implementation project, whether it is a small-scale, proof-of-concept effort by a single faculty member, or a larger department or campuswide initiative. By clearly identifying the stakeholders in a given context and then working through each of the steps in the framework shown in this chapter to design effective ePortfolio implementation tasks, project leaders can build a culture of collaboration and integration of effort in documenting learning. For faculty instructors in particular, this approach is useful in demonstrating that even efforts on a course-based scale can benefit from thinking more broadly about the stakeholder perspective and thus assist students to be more engaged and responsible learners.

Important Considerations

- Consider your learning outcomes in order to identify the stakeholders on your campus who might be interested in ePortfolios.
- Employ the design thinking methods to develop an iterative process for implementing ePortfolios that addresses stakeholder interests and needs.
- At all times, keep in mind the types of evidence that will be required to convince various stakeholders of the value of using ePortfolios as you evaluate the impact of your implementation project.

Designing Effective ePortfolio Learning Activities

Student engagement is one of the most important features of higher education today. As indicators like the National Survey of Student Engagement (NSSE) tell us, engaged students learn more because they participate in a variety of educationally purposeful activities (Kuh, 2003). Indeed, NSSE results have pointed to the most common approaches for engaging learners, which George Kuh and his colleagues refer to as "high-impact educational practices." When provided as opportunities in which students can participate both inside and outside the classroom, these practices allow students to connect in meaningful ways to course materials, and to transfer knowledge among learning contexts within the academic environment (e.g., courses and formal educational experiences), workplace (e.g., in cooperative educational placements and internships) and community (e.g., residence life, volunteer opportunities which may occur on or off campus, and service learning). Ideally, learners will connect all of these experiences and link them in a coherent way with who they are as learners. ePortfolios represent one way to facilitate this integration and support learners in making such connections.

Making connections among learning experiences, however, is not necessarily a natural part of what students come to colleges and universities knowing how to do. This requires an integration of experiences that needs to be scaffolded for students across the curriculum. The design of what Dee Fink (2003) refers to as "significant" learning experiences (see Figure 3.1) aligns well with the types of learning that research suggests is needed in higher education.

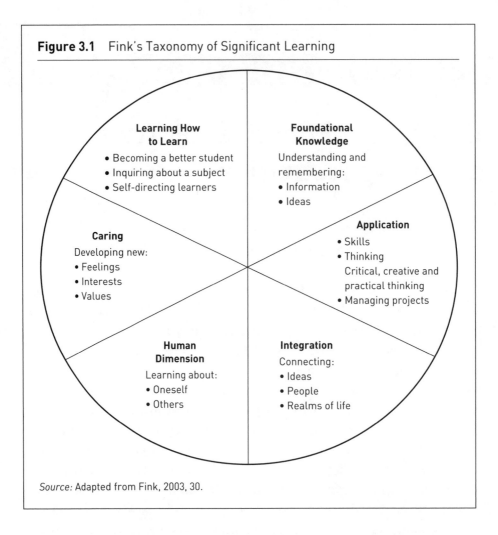

Figure 3.1 Fink's Taxonomy of Significant Learning

Learning How to Learn
- Becoming a better student
- Inquiring about a subject
- Self-directing learners

Foundational Knowledge
Understanding and remembering:
- Information
- Ideas

Caring
Developing new:
- Feelings
- Interests
- Values

Application
- Skills
- Thinking
  Critical, creative and practical thinking
- Managing projects

Human Dimension
Learning about:
- Oneself
- Others

Integration
Connecting:
- Ideas
- People
- Realms of life

Source: Adapted from Fink, 2003, 30.

For instance, a recent report from the Association of American Colleges and Universities (AAC&U) by the National Leadership Council for Liberal Education and America's Promise (LEAP) suggests that what is required in today's institutions of higher education is

> an approach to college learning that seeks to empower individuals and prepare them to deal with complexity, diversity, and change. This approach emphasizes broad knowledge of the wider world (e.g., science, culture, and society) as well as in-depth achievement in at least one specific field of study. It helps students develop a sense of social responsibility, strong

cross-disciplinary intellectual and practical skills (e.g., communication, ana-lytical and problem-solving skills), and a demonstrated ability to apply knowledge and skills in real-world settings. (2011, p. 3)

If this is the case, faculty instructors have a tall order to fill: learners need to be engaged in the disciplinary content and thinking that is important for understanding a specific field of study, but at the same time, they also require assistance from instructors to develop a more integrated way of viewing the world. To ensure that this synthesis occurs, instructors must think through the ways that course learning outcomes map to teaching and learning activities and to assessment and evaluation methods.

This process of aligning teaching and learning methods and assessment approaches with course learning outcomes is essential for designing learning activities that engage learners in an integrated and meaningful way (see Figure 3.2). The eight ePortfolio implementation issues outlined in Chapter Two are helpful in thinking through the design of engaging activities for documenting learning. In contrast, the six steps within the ePortfolio Implementation Framework—defining learning outcomes; identifying and understanding learners and stakeholders; designing learning activities; informing assessment of student learning; using ePortfolio tools and technologies; and evaluating the impact of your ePortfolio initiative—represent a more condensed and practical application of the eight broad issues that are comprehensively discussed in this chapter.

These eight issues speak to the integration that is necessary to develop responsible and engaged learners who are able to make connections between the disciplinary content, knowledge and skills in the classroom and their application in the "real" world (Chen and Penny Light, 2010).

1. Defining learning outcomes

2. Understanding your learners

3. Identifying stakeholders

4. Designing learning activities

5. Including multiple forms of evidence

6. Using rubrics to evaluate ePortfolios

7. Anticipating external uses of evidence

8. Evaluating the impact of electronic portfolios

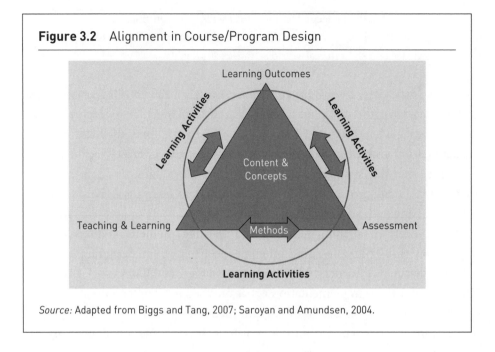

Figure 3.2 Alignment in Course/Program Design

Learning Outcomes

Learning Activities

Learning Activities

Content & Concepts

Teaching & Learning

Methods

Assessment

Learning Activities

Source: Adapted from Biggs and Tang, 2007; Saroyan and Amundsen, 2004.

Although these issues can inform strategies for engaging various stakeholders in an ePortfolio project, they are especially salient to instructional design and the scaffolding of integrative learning. Particular attention is paid to the ways in which instructors can engage learners in ePortfolio work to make connections between their various learning experiences as they document their learning and identity development. Instructional design activities for faculty instructors to assist in the process of designing significant, integrative approaches to learning are included, as well as examples of learning activities from different disciplines and student results.

AN INSTRUCTIONAL DESIGN FRAMEWORK FOR INTEGRATIVE LEARNING WITH ePORTFOLIOS

One of the main challenges for instructors when implementing any innovation in the classroom is achieving buy-in from the key stakeholders—students. Anyone who has ever tried something new in the classroom is well aware that if the activity is not tightly integrated with the teaching, learning, and assessment methods, it is doomed to failure (and sometimes even if it is so integrated). ePortfolios are no exception to this rule. Given this fact, our implementation issues for ePortfolio projects serve not only as a way of thinking through this approach of documenting learning, but also as an instructional design strategy. Each issue is outlined in more detail here, with particular attention paid to the important considerations that need to be addressed when implementing ePortfolios.

1. Defining Learning Outcomes

This is perhaps the most important issue in developing a plan for using ePortfolios whether in the classroom, in an entire program, or at the institutional level. ePortfolios offer many affordances for instructors who are looking to engage their learners more deeply with course content. However, thinking through exactly *how* that engagement will happen is a crucial step in the process of creating and implementing this pedagogical approach. For instance, you might ask yourself what type of learning experience you want students to have in your particular course or program? How will the ePortfolio be used to allow students to make connections to other instances of learning that they experience in other contexts? When they enter your classroom, will students already be thinking about how to connect the learning that happens in other contexts (e.g., academic, workplace, or community) to the learning that happens in your particular classroom? If so, how will that be documented in the ePortfolio? If not, what will you need to do to set them up for success?

The Association of American Colleges and Universities (AAC&U) has developed a set of essential learning outcomes that are particularly useful for initially thinking through this process. These outcomes include:

- Knowledge of human cultures and the physical and natural world which can occur in the study of the sciences and mathematics, social sciences, humanities, histories, languages and the arts;

- Intellectual and practical skills which include things like inquiry and analysis, critical and creative thinking, and effective communication skills;

- Personal and social responsibility including things like civic knowledge and engagement and ethical reasoning and action; and

- Integrated and applied learning, which includes synthesis and advanced accomplishment across general and specialized skills. (National Leadership Council for Liberal Education and America's Promise, 2007, 12)

ePortfolios can provide a space where students can document their ability to meet these outcomes through the artifacts that they select to include to demonstrate their skills and abilities. However, it is often difficult for learners to know which artifacts are most representative and effective for different readers of their ePortfolio. This is why clear learning outcomes are essential. One of the most important aspects of starting an ePortfolio initiative is to think through which of these outcomes will be most useful for your learners, depending on their developmental stage or the context. In other words, when determining your expectations of the levels of competency in your learning outcomes (which can potentially be assessed using rubrics, which are discussed in more detail in Chapter Six), it is important to take a developmental perspective of what might reasonably be expected of learners at that stage. For instance, you might consider whether you are teaching them at an introductory, intermediate, or advanced level. What other learning experiences might they be bringing with them—that is, what other learning might have shaped their knowledge or understanding of the content and skills you are teaching? As noted in Chapter Two, knowing who your stakeholders are is an important step in developing a program for documenting learning with ePortfolios.

Of course, outcomes that are not clearly articulated will be difficult for students to document. Therefore, it is important to think through the outcomes at the early stages of the implementation of the ePortfolio, by answering these questions:

- What are the learning outcomes or what will students know, understand, or be able to do at the end of this learning experience?

- How will students demonstrate that they have gained competency in the outcomes as articulated?

Keeping in mind the various essential learning outcomes as well as the importance of reflection in the process of documenting learning, it is critical to create outcomes that clearly articulate what students are expected to know and be able to do by the end of the learning experience. Useful for this process is Bloom's

Figure 3.3 Bloom's Taxonomy of the Cognitive Domain

Bloom's Taxonomy "Revised"	Verbs related to each learning level
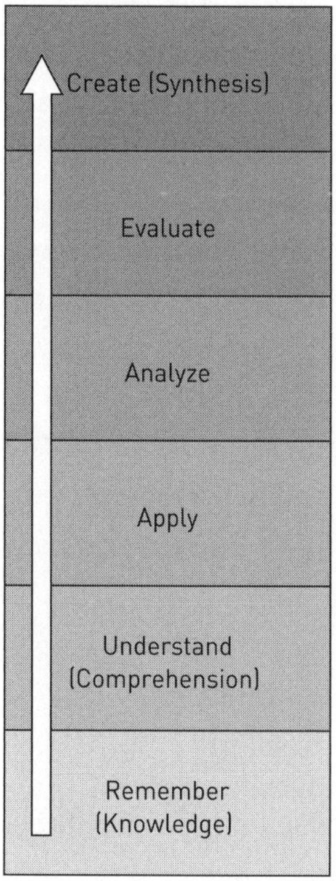 Create (Synthesis)	*Create* (Synthesis): compose, produce, design, assemble, create, prepare, predict, modify, tell, plan, invent, formulate, collect, generalize, document, combine, relate, propose, develop, arrange, construct, organize, originate, derive, write
Evaluate	*Evaluate:* judge, assess, compare, evaluate, conclude, measure, deduce, argue, decide, choose, rate, select, estimate, validate, consider, appraise, value, criticize, infer
Analyze	*Analyze:* analyze, compare, probe, inquire, examine, contrast, categorize, differentiate, investigate, detect, survey, classify, deduce, scrutinize, discover, inspect, dissect, discriminate, separate
Apply	*Apply:* apply, relate, develop, translate, use, operate, organize, employ, restructure, interpret, demonstrate, illustrate, calculate, show, exhibit, dramatize
Understand (Comprehension)	*Understand* (Comprehension): restate, locate, report, recognize, explain, express, identify, discuss, describe, review, infer, conclude, illustrate, represent, interpret, draw, differentiate
Remember (Knowledge)	*Remember* (Knowledge): know, identify, relate, list, define, recall, memorize, repeat, record, name, recognize, acquire

Source: Adapted from Bloom, 1956; Anderson and Krathwohl, 2000.

taxonomy as shown in Figure 3.3 (Bloom, 1956; Anderson and Krathwohl, 2000). The taxonomy of cognitive learning is one way to think through different levels of learning, and, therefore, different ways of articulating what students should do at a particular point in their learning career.

The taxonomy is a useful way of thinking through how to articulate the learning outcomes that you want your students to meet. This, of course, is an important practice for all instructors, whether or not they are using ePortfolios. ePortfolios provide opportunities for students to reflect on the material over the duration of the learning experience and then demonstrate how their thinking

Concept Mapping

1. Start with a free-writing exercise: What will your students know, understand, or be able to do at the end of your course?
2. Circle important words or phrases from your free-writing.
3. Create a concept map that visually represents the outcomes that you want students to achieve. This may take the form of a more traditional mind-map, or may be a metaphor for the learning experience you want students to have in your course.

can be applied elsewhere. By identifying learning outcomes and sharing them with students, instructors ensure that there are clear connections for the students between the course assignments and the course learning goals. In addition, clearly articulated learning outcomes allow the instructor to design effective learning activities that support students' achievement of these outcomes. Communicating the expectations for the course will enable the students to complete the requirements successfully. The concept map shown in Figure 3.4 was designed as a communication tool to help students to understand the process of "doing history." It is included on course outlines and maps to the learning outcomes articulated for those courses (see below).

Learning Outcomes for History   After successfully completing this course, students will have the ability to:

- Comprehend and critique theories of the history of sexuality and put them in historical context (historiography);
- Apply historical theories of sexuality in critical analyses of their own research topics;
- Explain how interpretation results from historical memory and historical lenses as evident in a variety of primary and secondary sources;
- Critically analyze a variety of historical sources to develop their own interpretation of a topic with a focus on historical memory as a key component of historical analysis;
- Reflect on and articulate the process and products of historical analysis through their own research projects;
- Work with others to foster a deeper understanding of the history of sexuality in community.

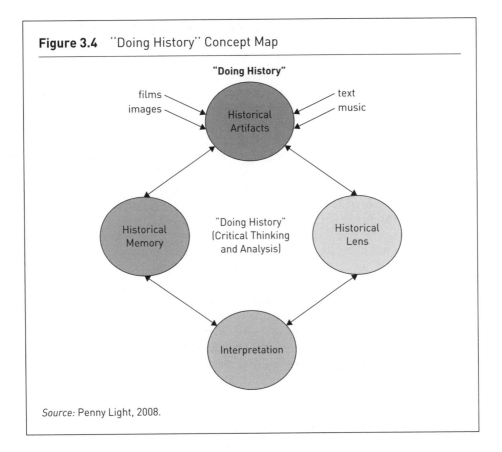

Figure 3.4 "Doing History" Concept Map

"Doing History"

films
images
text
music

Historical
Artifacts

Historical
Memory

"Doing History"
(Critical Thinking
and Analysis)

Historical
Lens

Interpretation

Source: Penny Light, 2008.

2. Understanding Your Learners

When the instructor has designed clear learning outcomes for their learners to address in their ePortfolios, it is important to identify who the learners are and their particular learning context, as they represent the most essential and critical stakeholder group (see Chapter Two). For our purposes here, the learner is the person who will be creating the ePortfolio and who will directly engage in a reflective process of collecting, selecting, and representing his or her work in this medium. It is important to clarify the concept of learner and his or her role up front because it is generally assumed that the author of the ePortfolio has ownership of both the format and the content and is responsible for deciding which pieces within the ePortfolio can be accessed by and shared with others (see Exhibit 3.1).

Exhibit 3.1 Creating a Learner Profile or Persona

Developing a profile or persona to represent your "typical" learner is helpful in planning activities that will be meaningful for them, as well as allow you to have empathy for them. Personas should include both demographic information, as well as a few personal attributes to help you think about your learner as a person. For example:

Stacy is a second-year student majoring in accounting. She has decided to take the History and Film course because it is on the list of electives from which she can choose, she likes to watch movies, and she thinks watching films for credit will assure her an "easy A." The last time she took history was in high school and she did not really enjoy it—it was a lot of information to remember and she hated learning about wars and politics. She spends a lot of her spare time keeping in touch with her friends on Facebook, although she does not really consider herself to be very technologically savvy.

A persona like this one can reveal to the faculty instructor a great deal about the learners they will be trying to engage with ePortfolios and can also help them to choose activities that will suit the overall learning outcomes of the course. Perhaps most important, keeping these learner characteristics in mind can inform how ePortfolio activities will be communicated to the students. In this case, given Stacy's belief that history courses are all about memorization, the instructor will need to clearly articulate and model the process of doing history so that this expectation can be overcome. In addition, Stacy indicates that she is not technologically savvy, so a plan for instruction and support for using the ePortfolio system will also need to be developed (Chen and Penny Light, 2010, 8–9).

Think through who your learners are:

- What characteristics might you use to describe them?
- What technologies are they comfortable using?

In addition, it is important that you not only understand their characteristics, skills, values, and interests, but also the context of their daily lives.

- Do your learners use technology a great deal, or a little?
- Do your learners use social networking tools to share their lives and experiences with friends, family, and colleagues?
- Are your learners new to the study in which you want to engage them? In other words, are they novices or are they more sophisticated learners who are looking to either reinforce or master the course materials?

A useful way of thinking through this is to consider again the concept of a "learning career" (Chen and Mazow, 2002; Chen and Penny Light, 2010) that maps the milestones that mark a student's progress through higher education and beyond (see Chapter Two). From the perspective of an instructor or program, the notion of a "learning career" allows us to identify whether the learning that happens in a particular course represents a minimum threshold that students will be required to meet in order to move forward to the next set of courses or other learning experiences. For learners, this can be an opportunity to evaluate what they know, understand, and are able to do at a particular moment in time in order to assess and plan for themselves what next steps they want to take in their learning; they may find that gaps exist in their knowledge and experience which they could take action to remedy.

3. Identifying Stakeholders

As discussed in Chapter Two, there are many stakeholders in any ePortfolio project; however, for the purpose of our definition in the context of instructional design, the stakeholders represent the audiences for the individual ePortfolios. Potential stakeholders include internal audiences, such as students, faculty instructors, administrators and other senior leaders, technical support staff, and administrative support staff, as well as external audiences, such as alumni, employers, mentors, peers, and family members. The role of stakeholders is a critical one, particularly in determining which factors and resources are necessary to ensure that the implementation is successful. Effectiveness and efficiency of ePortfolios converge around the needs of the stakeholders involved. For instance, faculty might use ePortfolios as a means to gather the evidence they need to understand what knowledge and skills students are taking away from their course, as well as how these competencies can be applied to other fields. For students, ePortfolios provide a space within which to consider the connections between the various learning experiences and to showcase their skills and abilities beyond the walls of the classroom. Therefore, it is important to think through the design of the ePortfolio within the context in which it is being used to ensure that it meets the needs of not only the individual learners but also the various other stakeholders that may be interested in the content contained therein.

If you think of the student experience not just in the context of your own course, but rather in the context of their entire learning career, it is possible to come up with a list of who else might be interested in the work that your students are doing, and they might help you move your initiative forward. For instance, the AAC&U report on the LEAP Vision for Learning (2011) points specifically to the needs of employers in our changing world. We can also think about the learning in one course or program and how that learning can provide evidence of whether students are meeting program learning outcomes, or even whether the learning that is happening in your specific project maps to learning that is expected to happen at a broader institutional or employment level. Considering all of these issues at the beginning of an ePortfolio implementation means that you will make the experience of creating an ePortfolio not only much richer for the learners involved, but also for the learning community in which this ePortfolio work is taking place.

4. Designing Learning Activities

Once your learners and stakeholders are identified, you can begin to design learning activities that will meet the learning outcomes that you have articulated. It is important to return to the learning outcomes or goals that the ePortfolio project was designed to address at all stages of the implementation process. The learning objectives are essential in order to define the expected knowledge, skills, and attitudes that students need to demonstrate in the assignment, course, or program as well as the level of required competency. A central feature of learning activities for ePortfolios is reflection. Reflective practices allow students to provide additional information on attitudes and the affective side of learning, while also encouraging the application and transfer of experiences and skills from one domain to another. The principle of alignment (see Figure 3.2) is also useful in this process. The learning outcomes should clearly align with the teaching, learning, and assessment methods that will be used to determine whether students have achieved a particular set of outcomes.

One of the key features of ePortfolios is the learner's ability to build a collection of artifacts that documents their competency in specific learning outcomes. This collection, however, should not just be seen as an archive of everything that the student has completed throughout various learning experiences. Rather, the learning activities should identify and define a structured time and space for the student to reflect on his or her education within the context of their ePortfolio. For instance, an instructor may ask students to create concept maps of particular content or topics discussed in a course at a given moment in time (see Figure 3.5).

Figure 3.5 Example Concept Map (History and Film)

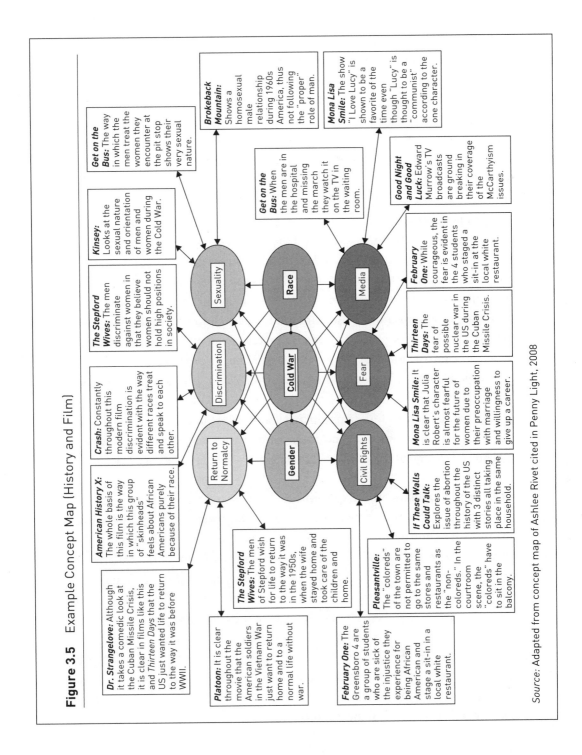

Source: Adapted from concept map of Ashlee Rivet cited in Penny Light, 2008

In the course where this concept map was created, an outcome for learners was to develop their historical thinking ability (critical thinking and analysis). Learners were asked to identify how the different films viewed in the course were connected to course themes and what the films contribute to our understanding of Cold War America. The maps were designed early in the term and then revised as the course unfolded. This example of a final concept map points to this student's emerging understanding that there can be multiple interpretations of the same topic. In this case, for example, her understanding that the films *Thirteen Days* and *Dr. Strangelove* both deal with the Cuban Missile Crisis, but from very different perspectives, can be observed.

Students might also think and reflect on the course materials in less traditional ways, such as video, digital, and audio recordings. Along with documenting their progress, reflective activities encourage learners to track their growth in defined areas and identify those that may need further development. In this way, the instructor is able to more closely monitor student progress toward achieving the goals of the course; this method also increases the number of opportunities to diagnose instructional challenges that could impede progress.

George Kuh has identified a number of high-impact educational practices, derived from his work with the National Survey on Student Engagement (NSSE), that are particularly useful when thinking about ePortfolios (Kuh, 2008). Following is a list of these practices and ideas for activities that can be used to allow students to document the learning that happens when they are engaged.

First-Year Seminars and Experiences   One way to bring small groups of students together with faculty or staff on a regular basis is by engaging learners in first-year seminars or experiences. When partnered with ePortfolios, these activities can be designed to place a strong emphasis on critical inquiry, frequent writing, information literacy, collaborative learning, and other skills that develop learners' intellectual and practical competencies. Evidence of the first-year experience can serve as a "benchmark" for where their learning began that can be reflected on over the course of their learning career. For instance, in the Library Field Trip activity described in Exhibit 3.2, first-year students learn together the skills necessary to develop effective research and critical thinking skills. They are provided with opportunities to debrief their experiences on the field trip and document their learning in their ePortfolios.

Exhibit 3.2   Library Field Trip

This activity was designed to engage learners in a first-year seminar course with the library to develop their research and critical thinking skills. The activity unfolds in these steps:

1. In the course, students read a series of "core texts" by authors from antiquity through to the modern period which address the theme "reflection and action." The core texts are Homer, *The Odyssey*; Augustine, *The Confessions*; Descartes, *Discourse on Method*; Hannah Arendt, *Eichmann in Jerusalem*. As each text is read, the class discusses it and the ways it addresses the theme, while also considering the applicability of the authors' discussion of reflection and action to everyday life and, in particular, to the life of a first-year student.

2. Students are provided minimal information about the authors at the beginning of the course and a conversation develops about the way that context is helpful in understanding an author and a text (first week of the course). As students come to agree as a group that this is important, the faculty instructor arranges a library "field trip." On the field trip, students are put into small groups (3–4 students) and are asked to find out about one of the authors. They are not given any guidance except to use the library and to keep track of the steps they took in order to find the information. The field trip lasts for one class period (80 min.). The students are also told that they need to present their findings to the rest of the class at the next meeting.

3. When students present their research, the class asks questions and discusses the usefulness of each group's approach. Inevitably, the groups set about the research process differently—some start online, some use encyclopedias, some use library staff as a resource, and so on. As such, they all gather quite different information about the author, which allows for a class discussion about the value of different types of research materials and also determining a "best approach" to doing library research. The instructor also makes connections between this activity and a small research project they will undertake later in the term.

4. Individual students are then responsible for documenting what they learned on the field trip in their ePortfolios, taking into account the ways that their group's approach was different from others and the lessons they learned about doing research that they will apply to their own individual research projects.

5. Students are asked to continue to reflect on their knowledge of the research process during the term, making connections between what happens in the reflection and action course, other classes they are taking, and how competency in conducting research might be applied beyond university.

One way to capture this benchmark and the shifts or changes in learning over time is to ask students to reflect on a particular topic several times during the term (as in the Library Field Trip example). These reflections at the beginning, middle, and end of the course can provide them with an opportunity to see how their learning has changed or developed during the course, and can also provide instructors with useful formative feedback in order to guide the learning of the students over the term.

In cases where collaborative learning is an important outcome, students may be asked to reflect on their group work experience and to document the learning that occurred as a result of that experience. Given the affordances of the electronic medium, a group of learners might decide to write a song or create a video of the learning that occurred within the group or a concept map that changed over the term.

Common Intellectual Experiences   In the past, learning around a core curriculum was one way that provided students with the ability to integrate their knowledge or to participate in a learning community. Today, general education programs that include advanced integrated studies expose students to common intellectual experiences. ePortfolios are wonderful ways of mapping the learning that happens throughout these programs by giving students an opportunity to document their competency around a variety of themes such as technology and society, global interdependence, and about how learning connects to a variety of curricular and co-curricular options that are available to them. For instance, affording a space for learners to consider how their residence life experience maps (or not) to core curricular topics provides an important opportunity for

Figure 3.6 Great Dialogues Course: Reflection and Action

In this first-year seminar, students are asked to make connections in their ePortfolios between the learning that happens in the course, their volunteer life, and their work lives in order to document their development as responsible citizens.

Source: http://eport.uwaterloo.ca/html/snapshot.php?id=20141818579418

students to begin the process of knowledge transfer among learning experiences that happen in different contexts (see Figure 3.6).

Learning Communities Learning communities provide a way for students to integrate their learning across courses and to involve a group of students in answering big questions that matter beyond the classroom. In learning communities students often explore a common topic or common readings through the lenses of different disciplines. Again, ePortfolios are a way for students to bring together those different learning experiences by providing an archive of learning artifacts. One of the key aspects of effective reflection, according to Carol Rodgers (2002), is this aspect of learning in community. In fact, she argues that this is one approach that John Dewey envisioned of reflection as a rigorous and scientific activity. In this way, ePortfolios can help to document the learning that happens in learning communities and to provide a space for students to actively integrate their learning experiences and share them with one another, or even with broader communities of peers, families, and employers.

Writing-Intensive Courses These courses emphasize writing at all levels of instruction across the curriculum, including final year projects. The effectiveness of writing across the curriculum has led to similar practices in areas such as quantitative reasoning, oral communication, information literacy, and even ethical inquiry. ePortfolios provide opportunities for students to document the learning that happens in those various instances and to bring together learning in one common space. Student reflections can also provide instructors with an important diagnostic tool to identify areas of weakness in a student's writing and to provide scaffolded feedback over the duration of a learning experience.

Learning Logs as a Diagnostic Writing Tool

In large introductory courses where students ought to be given opportunities to receive feedback on their writing in order to develop this skill, the numbers of students are often prohibitive to assigning papers. One way to overcome this challenge is to ask students to write short one- or two-page learning logs on the course content over the term and provide feedback to them on their writing. The advantages of using this approach are: (1) students can be provided with a rubric indicating what will be assessed (structure, grammar, spelling, reflective capacity); (2) instructors can use the rubric for quick and easy grading; (3) students receive feedback on their writing and have opportunities to improve over the term; (4) these provide space for reflection and opportunities for students to document learning; (5) student reflections provide instructors with formative feedback on the course.

Collaborative Assignments and Projects Collaborative learning combines two key goals: learning to work and solve problems in the company of others, and sharpening one's own understanding by listening seriously to the insights of others. This is particularly important when students have the opportunity to interact with learners who have different backgrounds and life experiences. Asking students to document the learning that happens in these collaborative projects is another way that ePortfolios can make space for students to reflect on what happens throughout their learning career.

Undergraduate Research Providing students with opportunities to participate in the research process is a way to involve them in thinking through how to ask and answer research questions, develop empirical observations, use cutting-edge technologies, and inspire the sense of excitement that comes from working to investigate important questions. These are important skills for today's learners, as they will go out into the world and be expected to approach problems with a critical eye. ePortfolios can be a central place to house students' experiences of the research process. Research ePortfolios ask students to document the important aspects of a particular research project including the theoretical lenses and methodological approaches used to study a particular topic.

Diversity and Global Learning Today, most students can expect to explore cultures and have life experiences, and world views that are different from other people they meet, learn and work with. Valuing the "other," therefore, is a central contemporary competency. ePortfolios can provide a way for students to document their experiences with other cultures whether this is through experiential learning in their own community, or through study abroad experiences. Blogs, for instance, are an interesting way for students to keep track of their experiences when they are studying abroad.

Service Learning and Community-Based Learning Field-based experiential learning with community partners is an instructional strategy for many courses today. Students are provided with direct experience when the issues they are studying in the curriculum unfold in a community-based setting. Important for this type of learning is the ability to transfer research to practice where students have the opportunity to apply what they are learning in real-world settings and reflect in a classroom setting on their service experiences. These particular approaches are important when thinking about ways to develop civic engagement and responsible citizenship.

Example Prompts for Documenting Collaborative Learning

1. What is one specific example of something that you learned from your group members that you would not have learned on your own?
2. What is one specific example of something that your group members learned from you that they would not have learned on their own?
3. Given this group experience, what will you do differently next time you work with a group? What will you do the same?

Beyond Borders Program (St. Jerome's University)

In the Beyond Borders program at St. Jerome's University, students participate in community service learning abroad. Students are expected to maintain blogs of their experiences where they reflect on what they are learning while away, and how it connects to their previous learning experiences and future plans for learning.

Virginia Tech SERVE program

At Virginia Tech, students can choose to live in a residence community where the focus is on fostering personal and civic growth. Students in the community study community development and social change theory while also engaging in a variety of service experiences, such as volunteering at local hunger relief agencies. Virginia Tech also offers a number of other living-learning communities in which students can choose to participate. This approach brings together both academic and community (cocurricular) learning.

Career Portfolios at Florida State University (FSU)

At FSU, the Career Portfolio program provides students with an opportunity to connect learning opportunities with employer needs and integrate curricular and cocurricular experiences (e.g., academic and career advising, courses, and service learning). The Career Portfolio was designed to provide an innovative Internet-based system to promote student learning, career preparation, and employment while also positively supporting student recruitment and retention. An important aspect of FSU's program is matching of ePortfolio goals to employer needs (Ford et al., 2009; Garis, 2007).

Internships and Cooperative Education Another common form of experiential learning is the internship, which can give students direct experience in a work setting usually related to their career interests. Internships provide students with the benefit of supervision and coaching from professionals in the field. ePortfolios can provide a way for students to reflect on their different experiences in the workplace and tie those experiences into learning that has happened in their courses and work programs.

Capstone Courses and Projects Capstone courses or projects allow students to bring together the learning that has happened over the course of their university degree. Important for these projects is the ability of students to integrate what they have learned and apply their skills and knowledge to new situations and environments. Again, ePortfolios can provide a means for students to selectively present artifacts from their archive of learning experiences to document the ways in which those experiences were meaningful for them and to share that meaning with instructors teaching the capstone courses as well as with peers and even family members.

In all of these examples the goal is deep rather than surface learning. On the whole, ePortfolio work can be incorporated into many of these high-impact educational practices to more naturally integrate a reflective component that serves to differentiate and distinguish their learning experiences.

5. Including Multiple Forms of Evidence

When designing learning activities, it is important to keep in mind the advantage of the ePortfolio for capturing evidence in a range of formats, including written documents, audio recordings, videos, and digital photographs. The result of using an ePortfolio is a much richer representation of the learners' experiences that is visible and accessible. Of course, the challenge for instructors in this medium is designing learning activities that support the development of the various types of evidence. Thoughtful attention to the many kinds of evidence that can be produced to meet the learning outcomes will make the implementation more effective for both instructors and learners, and more efficient in terms of grading and evaluating assignments. It is also important to consider the metrics for how that evidence will be assessed.

As shown in Table 3.1, researchers at George Mason University have explored whether patterns of evidence used in ePortfolios demonstrate learning more effectively than other types of learning (Cambridge et al., 2008, as cited in Chen and Penny Light, 2010).

Center for Service Learning at Indiana University-Purdue University Indianapolis (IUPUI)

Drawing upon the capstone model, IUPUI's Center for Service Learning (CSL) designed a civic learning pathstone portfolio experience, which identifies opportunities that could serve as base elements for a longitudinal "pathways" portfolio. The pathstone portfolio was structured to combine elements of process and learning portfolio design. Opportunities to pilot the combination of the portfolio tool and civic learning pathstone experiences were developed in two projects. In the Service Learning Assistant Scholarship Program Pilot, ePortfolios were introduced to undergraduate/graduate faculty and academic staff. In the Service Learning in First Year Success Seminars/Themed Learning Communities, which served as a bridge from the initial pilot work to a course-based intervention, the CSL collaborated with faculty to help them articulate Civic Learning outcomes in pathstone portfolio experiences. The outcomes of these pilots would eventually inform a developmental model of the Civic-Minded Graduate and the Civic Learning Pathway, which will be discussed further in Chapter Five.

6. Using Rubrics to Evaluate ePortfolios

Rubrics are a particularly powerful approach to understanding artifacts within the ePortfolio and relating them to the learning activities and learning outcomes

Table 3.1 An Emergent Typology of the Use of Evidence in ePortfolios

Dimensions	Frames
Characteristics of item used as evidence	**Agency** • Self-authored • Collaboratively authored (portfolio author and associates) • Other-authored **Media** • Media and modality of evidence (e.g., text, audio, image, streaming video, multimedia, etc.)
Purpose of incorporating evidence	**Rhetorical Function** • Intended (or deduced) function of the evidence (e.g., demonstrates or symbolizes) **Object** • Evidence reflects author's knowledge, skills, character traits, beliefs, goals, or identifications
Characteristics of associated learning activity	**Sponsorship** The activity is: • Institutionally sponsored (curricular, cocurricular, community organizations, etc.) • Self-sponsored • Unsponsored **Participation** Evidence indicates: • Individual participation • Group activity • Larger community/associational activity

Source: Adapted from Cambridge et al., 2008, and cited in Chen and Penny Light, 2010.

articulated to students at the beginning of a learning experience. Rubrics describe what is valued and rewarded for a given activity, and they foster greater transparency and accountability. When partnered with ePortfolio work, this approach provides a robust framework for assessing the many dimensions of learning both in a single learning experience, and through and across the curriculum and cocurriculum over time.

There are many different examples of rubrics that can be found online that can be modified to suit the learning activities that you may be designing. The Association of American Colleges & Universities (AAC&U) has undertaken a national project to develop rubrics through their campus-based Valid Assessment of Learning in Undergraduate Education project (Rhodes, 2010). These rubrics, which correspond to the learning outcomes identified in their LEAP initiative, provide campuses, departments, disciplines, and programs with a useful starting point for the discussion of specific criteria that can be used to judge the quality of student work in light of specific outcomes, such as integrative learning and critical thinking. See http://www.aacu.org/value/rubrics/pdf/integrativelearning.pdf. The rubrics are discussed in Chapter Six.

Any rubric that is created can be shared with students at the beginning of the learning experience when the learning outcomes are communicated so that they understand what is expected of them. This allows students to plan to incorporate various aspects of their learning into their ePortfolio activities and provides a scaffold for them to develop their knowledge, skills, and abilities. Rubrics are also useful for instructors. Building a rubric helps to operationalize the learning outcomes in a concrete way and forces us to be clear about what it is that we want our students to achieve in a particular learning context.

7. Anticipating External Uses of Evidence

Although learning activities created within a particular learning context are designed to allow learners to develop particular abilities, it is also important to consider how the artifacts that are captured in a student's ePortfolio might inform departmental, programmatic, or institutional learning. These artifacts can often provide useful information for departmental and program evaluation but may also be useful for wider institutional research or accreditation efforts. For instance, a campus administering the National Survey of Student Engagement (NSSE) might find student ePortfolios a useful link to understanding the ways that students are engaged (or not) on a campus. Other institutional data, such as pass/fail rates and retention, qualitative feedback from faculty and students, and quantitative surveys of courses, programs, and departments might all be used in connection with student ePortfolio artifacts to gauge the effectiveness of a department, program, or even an entire institution in its ability to train students (Chen and Penny Light, 2010, 21). The issue of what constitutes authentic evidence of student learning has become more critical as of late given the findings of Arum and Roksa (2011), who analyzed survey and transcript data from over 2,300 students who took the Collegiate Learning Assessment (CLA) at a range of four-year colleges and universities. They found that "gains in critical thinking, complex reasoning, and writing skills (i.e., general collegiate skills) are either exceedingly small or empirically nonexistent for a large proportion of students" (Social Science Research Council, 2011). Transcripts and standardized tests such as the CLA certainly represent one view of student learning, but faculty instructors may also want to think beyond the learning that is happening in one context (such as a course) and consider how a broader folio thinking approach could also be useful for more comprehensive institutional and educational goals. We discuss some possible ways to partner with other campus stakeholders in greater detail in Chapter Five.

8. Evaluating the Impact of ePortfolios

It is important to plan for the use of ePortfolios and the activities that will be used to document learning. Equally critical, however, is considering early on how you will determine whether the initiative has been successful. Considering how to evaluate whether the ePortfolio intervention has met the intended goals or outcomes identified at the beginning of the project is as essential as defining the learning outcomes themselves. We discuss the ways to evaluate impact in more detail in Chapter Nine, but it is necessary to note here the need to think about what types of evidence will be needed to document the success of the initiative in terms of the goals of the project, the impact on teaching and learning, the satisfaction of the various stakeholders, the quality of the technological approach implemented, and the availability of resources and support. Thinking through these issues as you develop your ePortfolio project will allow you to capture the evidence needed to formatively inform ongoing improvement of the initiative.

All of these steps are necessary for instructors to consider when working to engage learners using ePortfolios. The hallmark of any ePortfolio initiative is the ability of students to make connections between their various learning experiences as they document their learning. This engagement, however, does not happen organically. Effective and well-designed activities are essential to this process, not only to ensure that learners are being supported and encouraged to make those connections, but also to foster buy-in among these important stakeholders. Mindfully thinking through the learning outcomes that are to be achieved and then designing learning and assessment strategies that align with them ensures that significant, integrative learning will be the result.

Important Considerations

- Clearly define your learning outcomes and consider how the ePortfolio can help students document their learning to meet those outcomes.
- Communicate! Students need to understand why they are creating ePortfolios. Open a dialogue about documenting learning at the beginning of the class and keep it open. This is a great way to get feedback about what is and is not working.
- Keep it simple! Don't try to change your entire course all at once. Begin with small steps—try changing one or two assignments at first. This way, you can monitor the effectiveness of the approach and modify as needed.
- Systematically examine previously used assignments from a past offering of the class and look at the work products and artifacts that came out of those assignments; from those, select the artifacts that would make for a strong ePortfolio.
- Align the ePortfolio activities with the assessment strategy you will use to evaluate the students' learning—be sure to clearly communicate to the learners the metrics you will use to evaluate their level of success and accomplishment. This could be an activity that you engage them in—such as asking them to either self-assess or assess each other's ePortfolios and determine to what extent a particular learning outcome has been met.
- Plan-Monitor-Control: This is an iterative process that requires ongoing management throughout the implementation. Given the ability of ePortfolios to facilitate formative as well as summative feedback, be sure to track how things are unfolding throughout the semester and modify your plans if needed.

PART 2

Creating and Implementing ePortfolios

This section focuses on the practice of creating and implementing ePortfolios by outlining the ways that different stakeholders can be engaged with ePortfolios. Each chapter explores important considerations for the various stakeholders through examples of current practices from college and university campuses.

We begin with perhaps the most important stakeholder for faculty instructors to consider: students. We explore the ways that instructors can make a compelling case to students of the importance and benefits of ePortfolios for them as learners. Consideration is then given to other important campus partners for the promotion of civic engagement and responsible citizenship, for making connections beyond the classroom (for instance, in the workplace), and for supporting assessment efforts.

4

Engaging Today's Learners: Students and ePortfolios

For faculty instructors, the benefits of ePortfolios for students are often easily recognizable: at a very basic level, they allow learners to make connections among varied learning experiences and transfer knowledge and skills to new contexts and situations. This approach, particularly when it capitalizes on the features of ePortfolios together with a culture of folio thinking, can promote deep and integrative learning. For students, however, the value of ePortfolios and folio thinking may be unclear. Students may initially assume that the use of ePortfolios in a course or program is simply a new and faddish approach to teaching and learning. Indeed, without effectively communicating the purpose of ePortfolios and the benefits that ePortfolios are intended to produce for them, students may resist the approach, thereby making it challenging for them to really capitalize on those benefits. In order to effectively frame the purpose of using ePortfolios to students, you must have a comprehensive understanding of who your learners are. The goal for any instructor is to make the case for ePortfolios with a compelling argument that specifically addresses students' needs and concerns. In other words, the message should be about the ways that ePortfolios are personally significant and relevant to students both in the context of the course, program, or institution but also to their overall learning, individual goals, and identity development. This chapter discusses some strategies to foster student buy-in and provides several examples of activities to engage students in the folio thinking process.

UNDERSTANDING TODAY'S STUDENTS

Whether the students are adult learners returning to school to prepare for a career change or traditional 17- to 22-year-olds who exemplify the qualities of the Net Generation (Educause, 2005; Oblinger, 2003; Pew Research Center, 2010), Digital Natives (Prensky, 2001), and Generation M(ultitasking) (The Henry J. Kaiser Family Foundation, 2010) learners, having a sense of students' characteristics, priorities, and lives both inside and outside the classroom is critical to the design of any ePortfolio initiative. The following is a summary of some of the perceptions of ePortfolios that may be held by students. These questions have been gleaned from "anti-ePortfolio" opinion pieces written for student newspapers.

- Will anyone look at this? Will employers and graduate schools actually read my ePortfolio? Will they care to read a paper that I wrote in a freshman philosophy course?

- Why is the ePortfolio now considered evidence of my learning? Aren't my degree and my grades enough?

- Why do I need to share what I do? Why should there be a "social" aspect to my academic efforts?

- Who is reviewing what is in my ePortfolio? How rigorous is the evaluation process?

- Why should students who are not in fields that require ePortfolios keep and update an ePortfolio?

- Why should this be a requirement of all students? Why can't there be a choice?

- It's a lot of work. Why is this worth my time?

It should be noted that some of these concerns are expressed by some faculty instructors as well, particularly with respect to perceptions of what typically constitutes evidence of learning, namely test scores, grades, diplomas, and degrees. The vocabulary used to describe ePortfolios to students is an important consideration—in one of the editorial pieces, the author expressed sarcasm towards terms such as "learning outcomes," "core competencies," and "mastery." For many students, these phrases represent academic jargon and are not very helpful as they struggle with real-world concerns of figuring out how to pay for their college degree and what kind of job they will be able to get after graduation. In many ways, this disconnect parallels ongoing debates about the value of a liberal arts education, particularly for students who are increasingly vocationally oriented in their goals for their undergraduate education and who often see this period as merely a stepping stone to their future profession. Given this careerist mindset, many of these students may find the idea of developing "core competencies" not overly helpful to them and their future. The challenge is ensuring that learners understand *how*, *why*, and *where* the ePortfolio process and product will be useful. Careful thought must be given to how to communicate the value of this new approach in a language that is meaningful and relevant to students and their needs at the various milestones in the learning career that begins in college or university and beyond.

STRATEGIES TO FRAME ePORTFOLIOS FOR STUDENTS

Given students' concerns about the value of ePortfolios and their "return on investment," the following are some strategies for addressing and responding to some of the questions posed above.

- *Will anyone look at this? Will employers and graduate schools actually read my ePortfolio? Will they care to read about a paper that I wrote in a freshman philosophy course?*

Although the one-page résumé will undoubtedly still be what employers will want to look at first when narrowing down their candidate pool, the ePortfolio is something that would be of interest when prospective employers are trying to decide which applicant to hire among their top three finalists. Increasingly, the first thing recruiters do is to google applicants; it can be quite valuable to have their search bring up a formal ePortfolio that carries the credibility of an academic institution. Florida State University's Career ePortfolio sponsored by their Career Center has conducted surveys of employers who indicate that online career ePortfolios are useful in the recruiting process. Though employers and graduate schools may not care about any individual paper or product, they are interested in students' ability to demonstrate written communication skills with actual writing samples and being able to see growth and improvement over time, for example, from first-year writing to a senior honors thesis.

- *Why is the ePortfolio now considered evidence of my learning? Aren't my degree and my grades enough?*

As the official record of the educational experience, a student's academic transcript simply lists the classes taken and grades received. It represents the education that was defined by the institution and delivered to the student but does not always acknowledge what the student got out of his or her classes and other kinds of cocurricular and extra-curricular experiences such as studying abroad, community service, co-ops, and internships that might have occurred on and off campus. The ePortfolio platform offers an opportunity for students to include and share these informal experiences and achievements that might otherwise have been overlooked but which are often quite significant and memorable in influencing students' personal interests and growth, and in defining their passions. Thus, the degree and grades are not enough because, frankly, they are incomplete and limited in their ability to fully represent the holistic picture of an undergraduate education as it develops both inside and outside the classroom.

- *Why should students who are not in fields that require ePortfolios keep and update an ePortfolio? It's a lot of work. Why is this worth my time?*

Though some fields such as teacher education, architecture, graphic design, and writing and rhetoric have a culture of portfolios and reflection, the concept may be unfamiliar to professions such as engineering and the social sciences. However, increasing external pressures related to accountability and institutional accreditation have instigated the development of a culture of assessment where more authentic evidence of student learning is not only expected but actually mandated by the institution, the system, and often the state. For example, ABET, the accrediting body for engineering programs, has also defined a set of program educational outcomes that includes both technical and nontechnical (or "soft") skills that faculty are expected to teach and measure. It is often difficult for students to understand how these kinds of ePortfolios can be of use to them and, as a result, they simply treat it as another requirement to check off and "get out of the way." However, students can benefit from an ePortfolio requirement in multiple ways as a product (to show prospective employers as discussed) and also a process for understanding and gaining practice articulating and reflecting upon their achievements and how they fit together, as they might be asked to do in a job or graduate school interview. The following example from Clemson University illustrates how Jennifer Johnson, one of the winners of their annual ePortfolio contest in 2011, describes the rationale behind her ePortfolio:

> My ePortfolio site is a varying collection of artifacts demonstrating the skills and knowledge I have gained while attending Clemson University's College of Engineering & Science. Within my ePortfolio, you can track my academic development by exploring such links as my freshman General Engineering project, my senior Civil Engineering Capstone Design Project, and even my General Education Competencies highlighting my entire educational experience. Throughout my site, you will also find clear evidence of why I believe I have developed into a competent Transportation Engineering professional. As a senior with graduation quickly approaching, I have submitted my ePortfolio to possible employers for them to review such artifacts as my technical research papers, AutoCAD and GIS software skills, past internship and professional organization experiences, and other valuable resources like resumes, references, and honors/awards that are beneficial in "selling" myself throughout the interview process. My ePortfolio has received an exceptional amount of positive feedback from both professors and industry leaders as I have used it as a primary source of reference in applying for graduate school fellowships and even full-time jobs in Transportation Engineering. [http://www.clemson.edu/academics/programs/eportfolio/news.html]

THE ePORTFOLIO AS A "CABINET OF CURIOSITIES"

The concept of a "learning career" introduced in Chapter Two provides an overall perspective of where ePortfolios could be implemented within the existing educational trajectory. It is also entirely reasonable to consider experimenting with ePortfolios in an individual course, workshop, or program as a strategy to engage learners in a more meaningful way. As an instructor, you may consider how the learning experience you are designing fits within the student learning career at your institution and how an ePortfolio component can take advantage of existing milestones where students may already be documenting and reflecting upon their learning. In short, consider what value an ePortfolio can bring—whether it's streamlining and increasing the efficiency of activities that are already ongoing or contributing an innovative perspective and opportunity that will provide new insights, knowledge, and understanding of students' learning careers within the context of their broader educational and vocational goals.

Documenting a Learning Career in a "Cabinet of Curiosities"

Inevitably, students will compare the learning ePortfolio to their Facebook or LinkedIn accounts. Though it is possible to create an ePortfolio within these popular social networking platforms, it is important to reiterate that the focus of the learning ePortfolio is to document the development of an intellectual identity, not a social identity. Macaulay Honors College of the City University of New York system uniquely characterizes the student's learning career and the ePortfolio as a "cabinet of curiosities" by framing these concepts in the following way:

> Think of all the work you do while you're a student at Macaulay. Assignments for classes, projects, a thesis, essays, photography, videos, musical performances, websites, blogs, wikis, mathematical formulae, scientific research or experiments, short stories, poetry ... even more. Then think beyond that. Think of the other kinds of work you also do, that might be less formal, or less "official." Conversations with friends, interesting websites that have influenced your thinking and learning, books you've read on your own, places you've visited, souvenirs, emails ... and even more than that, too.
>
> All of these are "artifacts" of your thinking, your learning, yourself while you're a Macaulay Honors College student. If you could put it all together, in a cabinet, or a room (or a huge building!), you would have a cabinet of curiosities (a *wunderkammer*). It could be the museum of you—and you could invite people in to take a look. You could decide which rooms in your museum would be good for showing to which audience, depending on what you wanted them to know about you. You could keep some rooms private, only for you, and you could have other rooms that you showed only to special people.
>
> Even better, you could spend some time by yourself or with a few friends or colleagues, walking through the rooms, looking over all your artifacts, and

thinking about what they mean to you, what they show about you. And as time goes by you might have different thoughts about each artifact, because when you learn more, you see things in a different way. And when you show your artifacts to friends and colleagues, they might be able to point out things that you missed yourself—things you didn't know you were learning. Then when you show the rooms in your museum to other people, you could tell them some of what you thought—you could guide them through your museum, explaining why you chose to include the artifacts, describing how you got them, and how they relate to other objects. You might even want to move things around, or make new rooms, or make a new map that shows how different rooms or shelves relate to each other.

And in a way, that's what an ePortfolio is. It's a digital representation of your cabinet of curiosities, your *wunderkammer,* your museum of you. You get to build it, put your artifacts into it, design it, redesign it, think about it, show it to other people, get their comments, and tell them what you think.

The analogy of the student as curator of a collection of digital artifacts is a useful framing to communicate to students their critical role in selecting, preserving, certifying, and presenting these assets.

ENGAGING STUDENTS AS ePORTFOLIO CONSULTANTS AND CAMPUS ADVOCATES

Another approach to fostering student engagement with ePortfolios is to build a student cohort of ePortfolio consultants who can advocate for ePortfolios to both students and faculty on campus. The concept of the ePortfolio consultant has worked successfully at numerous institutions including LaGuardia Community College and State University New York (SUNY) at Stony Brook. Some of the responsibilities of a cohort of student ePortfolio support staff might include:

- Developing a comprehensive understanding of folio thinking and the value of reflection in the creation of ePortfolios
- Acquiring technological expertise in the campus ePortfolio tool(s) and creating relevant resources, workshops, handouts, videos, and other training materials for faculty and students
- Building their own ePortfolios

- Informing strategic planning for the ePortfolio initiative with respect to spreading the word about ePortfolios and engaging students, faculty, staff, and other possible constituents (e.g., alumni, prospective employers) on and off campus

SUNY Stony Brook's ePortfolio initiative is housed within their Faculty Center which is part of the broader Teaching, Learning, and Technology organization focused on supporting faculty teaching and student learning on campus. As a result, student workers are not only trained on how to use the technology but they also become knowledgeable about the theories and literature behind ePortfolios and folio thinking.

SUNY Stony Brook's ePortfolio work continues to emphasize the importance of student involvement in all aspects of its initiative as Nancy Wozniak, Stony Brook's ePortfolio Program Manager, states: "Authentic learning through the use of ePortfolios must be student-driven on campus. Our students respond to recognition and awards.... It's not an ePortfolio without the reflection and students take ownership of their ePortfolio and learning when they understand and include reflection" (Digication, 2011). Student ePortfolios that are selected as model ePortfolios are featured on the banner of the campus directory, on the Digication ePortfolio vendor's featured site, the Teaching Learning and Technology homepage, and via social media through Twitter, LinkedIn, and Facebook web sites that are shared with the public. Students also receive a certificate and letter of recognition and are also invited to share their ePortfolios at the university's annual spring teaching colloquium.

The criteria that student ePortfolios must meet in order to be featured in Stony Brook's "Gallery of Stars" is shown in Exhibit 4.1. The italicized notes have been added to highlight several key aspects of these recommendations. This checklist is useful in how it communicates what characterizes a good ePortfolio and encourages students to strive to meet these standards for excellence.

MODELING REFLECTION IN COURSE-BASED INTERVENTIONS

Although reflection is certainly an essential component of folio thinking, it is also widely acknowledged to be a skill that needs to be taught, modeled, and practiced by students in order to be truly effective while creating their ePortfolio.

Exhibit 4.1 What Makes It a Model Checklist?

By Nancy Wozniak and Sourav Tamang

Steps to a Model ePortfolio:

1. **Think about your work and experiences. Choose the best!** You want to assemble a collection of works that demonstrate and showcase your talents and abilities in all areas of your life. You're talented. Let the world know. An ePortfolio will help as you transition from your Stony Brook academic career to applying for graduate school and searching for a job in your chosen professional field. Your ePortfolio gives you dimension.

   Notes: An ePortfolio that is designed for external or professional review is very different from a personal, developmental ePortfolio that might contain work in progress and exploration of possible majors and careers. Many ePortfolio tools allow students to create either different views or even completely independent ePortfolios that are tailored to specific audiences (e.g., a prospective employer, graduate school, family, and friends).

2. **You MUST have an About Me or Bio category**. Composing your About Me doesn't have to be a long, painful process.

   Notes: The value of the introductory About Me page is not to be underestimated. A simple photo along with some background information can go a long way to connect a faculty member with who a student is.

3. **Categorize, Post, and Display** your showcase assignments, projects, activities, and experiences (known as "artifacts").

   Notes: Relating back to the first point, over the course of an academic term or even across an undergraduate learning career, students will amass a collection of artifacts. Many ePortfolio tools have features such as tagging or visualization tools that can help the ePortfolio owner organize their artifacts so that he or she can be selective in deciding which artifacts to feature, depending on the audience.

4. **Check Your Grammar!** Poor grammar and sentence structure take away from your creative and professional image. Think about your impression of the author of a paper riddled with spelling errors and broken sentence structure. Keep your writing conversational and grammatically correct. Use a spell checker. Have a buddy proofread your writing. You'll improve your writing style when you read others' writing.

   Notes: Like the following point about appropriate media, this recommendation about grammar and language emphasizes keeping in mind the potential audience viewing this ePortfolio and what conclusions they may draw about you from your ePortfolio.

5. **Add Media.** Images and video make your ePortfolio interesting and invite others to browse and read about your work. This isn't Facebook. This is a professional representation of you. Keep the media professional. Ask yourself, can I show this image to a future employer or my mom?

   Notes: Both points 4 and 5 emphasize the professional nature of a learning ePortfolio that carries the name and logo of their college or university. Unlike a personal web site or blog, the "brand" of the institution does carry some recognition and credibility that could differentiate this student from others who do not have a formal ePortfolio.

6. **Reflect!** This is the final and most important step. When you take the time to post a reflection on an artifact showcased in your ePortfolio, you demonstrate your reasoning and critical thinking abilities. You show deeper levels of your communication, creative, and leadership abilities. Your reflection shows a higher order of thinking on your part. Reflection completes the metacognitive process (making sense, self-analysis, and reflection . . . thinking about how you think) and helps you to make connections between learning and growth experiences in all areas of your life. Let's face it, posted reflections are impressive and allow others to view your multifaceted talents and abilities. After all, your ePortfolio is the best of you and you're amazing!

When writing a reflection on an assignment or learning experience, keep it simple. It doesn't need to be an essay. Ask yourself one or two of these reflection prompts about your assignment, course, project, program, or experience:

1. What did you learn?
2. What about this assignment or program was most useful to you?
3. What would you recommend to others about getting involved in this project or program? What suggestions would you offer?
4. What area in your life was strengthened or improved by the project or program?
5. List the ways you have grown as a result of this assignment, course or program?
6. What problems did you encounter? What risks did you take?
7. What experience in this program or assignment of this course demonstrated your strengths and talents and why?
8. If you had it to do all over again, would you? Why?

Notes: Although reflection is a separate step here, it is also implicit in the folio thinking process of creating an ePortfolio. Dr. Lee Shulman, former president of The Carnegie Foundation for the Advancement of Teaching and professor emeritus from the Stanford School of Education, referred to the selection of what to put into an ePortfolio and what to exclude as an "act of theory" (Shulman, 1998). Certainly, reflective prompts are a useful guide for students who are new to the folio thinking culture but recognize that reflection is an inherent and essential aspect of the entire process of ePortfolio creation.

7. **To receive full recognition of your model ePortfolio,** you must have your ePortfolio and the key categories set to Public View, such as, Welcome, About Me, Showcase Artifacts (course assignments, projects, activities, programs) with Reflections, CV or Resume. You know not to reveal too much about yourself. Show your talents, strengths, and abilities without posting personal identifiers and information.

Notes: Many ePortfolio tools have various permission settings for the ePortfolio with the basic premise being that students own the ePortfolio and they decide with whom they want to share their ePortfolio. Certainly, if an ePortfolio is part of a course then the student would be required to share it with the instructor and possibly their classmates. The above suggestion acknowledges that some students, in spite of their familiarity with technology, will still need guidance as to what's appropriate and not appropriate to share in their professional learning ePortfolio.

The following are two course-based examples that build and expand upon the ePortfolio concept in order to more actively and deeply engage students in both reflection and the learning process.

Digital Story as ePortfolio

The Student Wiki Interdisciplinary Group of Queensborough Community College in New York has built partnerships between students in English and Basic Educational Skills courses with those in the Education, Nursing, Social Sciences, and Speech/Theatre disciplines. These students follow a clearly articulated reflection cycle that guides student teams in the creation of a digital story.

Inspired by John Dewey's claim (1934) that reflection occurs as a process as the individual makes form out of the disparate elements of experience, the Queensborough team created a reflection cycle of eight individual stages in an effort to make the process visible and transparent to students (Darcy and Cuomo, 2010):

Queensborough Community College's Reflection Cycle

1. *Reflecting on community:* Threshold Experience—recognizing the students' meaning-making practices and helping them see the relationship to disciplinary discourse

2. *Reflecting on borders:* Negotiating the Borders of Disciplinary Discourse by communicating across disciplinary boundaries

3. *Reflecting on collaboration:* Mutual Gift Giving through the selection and examination of web "objects" and the relationship of writing to various multimedia modes

4. *Reflecting on choice:* Selecting and Storyboarding—deliberating on selections and sequencing choices to create a narrative

5. *Reflecting on different ways of knowing:* Integrating Voice with Visual Knowledge and allowing for rich tensions between different ways of integrating knowledge

6. *Reflecting on dissemination:* Producing and Distributing by becoming a producer of knowledge and developing agency in relation to the audience

7. *Reflecting on reception:* Presenting to Audience by becoming aware of the relation between the public and private through the braiding and weaving of personal stories in relation to other stories

8. *Assessing reflection:* Part of the Reflection Cycle Itself—integrating an assessment component that includes online surveys conducted at various points during the reflection cycle in order to raise student awareness and demonstrate student growth via this process

One example of how this process works begins with the following prompts from which a composition student writes a narrative essay about a significant learning experience:

Think about that memory of the learning experience. Describe it carefully.

Describe the person who is with you at the time.

Describe a dilemma associated with this memory and the change.

Describe the tentative resolution.

Describe how you changed the way you imagined the future.

As the essay is revised and refined, it is shared with students from the other courses who may offer "gifts" in various media including music, art, quotations, or cartoons in the wiki environment which is structured to facilitate the ePortfolio activity. In one instance, the essay was shared with an acting student who in turn performed the composition. Seeing one's written words come alive through performance was inspiring and moving for the essay author. The concept of "gift giving" resonated with students in multiple ways and influenced their views on group work, information processing, the role of media and the Internet in their learning, and interdisciplinary work. The opportunity to collaborate and communicate through these multimedia presentations was deeply engaging for many students and preliminary findings suggest a positive impact on retention rates for students in the project cohort.

The implications for faculty and instructors is to consider reflection as not just a single task that can be checked off and completed but as an iterative process that is revisited, revised, and reiterated as the student grows and as a project activity such as the digital story activity evolves during the course. The opportunity to employ cross-disciplinary and multimedia approaches in an integrative fashion models the ePortfolio process and engages students in iterative practice of these ideas not once, but multiple times.

Communicating What Is a "Good" Reflection to Students

The issue of what exactly constitutes "good" reflection is one that continues to be discussed and debated within the ePortfolio community. Much of the discussion comes down to how to design and craft a reflective prompt that leads to deeper and more meaningful reflections, rather than superficial and cliché comments that may be wordy and verbose but reveal little about what students actually learned. Observations of this occurrence led to an experiment conducted within a freshman design engineering seminar at Stanford University (Chen, Cannon, Gabrio, and Leifer, 2005). Supported by a grant from the National Science Foundation, researchers evaluated the weekly reflections submitted by students commenting on their individual and group experiences in their team projects. Results from these analyses showed that similar phrases were often used, perhaps attributable to the fact that students were writing their reflections at the last minute and not considering the broader implications and takeaways of their experiences. These oft-used phrases were summarized and then presented to students in subsequent iterations of the course as a conversation starter. These phrases are jokingly referred to as the "Taboo Phrases of Reflection," and though students are not forbidden from using them, their usefulness and significance are limited if meaningful reflection about the design process and teamwork is the desired outcome.

Taboo Phrases About Individual Tasks

- "very productive and effective"
- "insightful"
- "interesting"
- "creative"
- "put my creativity to the test" and other clichés like it
- "tried very hard"
- "which I thought was great"
- "I learned so much ..."
- "... learn a lot ..."
- "so much"

- "I learned that things don't always happen the way you plan them"
- "not that much I can say I wish had gone differently"
- "we needed more time"
- "went pretty well"
- "running pretty smoothly"
- "most important thing I learned along the way"
- "I learned how to think . . ."/ "I learned more about how to design . . ."
- "I wish I had put more time into . . ."
- "much more engaging"
- "think outside the box" and clichés like it
- "work more efficiently"
- "allowed us to look at design in a new way"
- just paraphrasing the words on the assignment sheet
- in general, avoid clichés or common sentences in responses
- excuses (for illness, business, or whatever) don't need to be in the reflection

Taboo Phrases About Group Work
- "everyone worked hard to meet"
- "discussed our plans thoroughly"
- "different perspectives and ideas"
- "open-minded"
- "workload was divided evenly"
- "achieved our goals"
- "everyone played an integral role" / "everyone had an equal voice"
- "everyone worked well together"
- "communicate well with your group"
- "listen to others"
- "work effectively in a group"
- "I feel our group did a good job of . . ."

- "improve on working together"

- "two heads are better than one" or any cliché like it.

- "I liked working with a team"

In sharing this list with the students, they were encouraged to consider how these phrases could be used more effectively, precisely, and thoughtfully, typically by connecting a phrase such as "this project put my creativity to the test" with some kind of example, a description, or some other form of evidence to illustrate and expand upon how a particular project challenged one's creative abilities. Engaging students in conversation around this list and emphasizing the

Table 4.1 Implications for Using ePortfolios with Student Stakeholders

Implementation Step	Guiding Questions
Learning Outcomes	Given the learning outcomes for the institution, department, program (such as general education), what are students' understanding of these outcomes and the relevance of these outcomes to their education, their courses, and their future careers? How are these outcomes framed and communicated to the students?
Stakeholders	For students, engaging external stakeholders who can lend credibility to the ePortfolio effort is important. Who else can you involve in your ePortfolio initiative, e.g. prospective employers, graduate school admissions, alumni?
Learning Activities	How do the learning outcomes for the institution, department, or program (such as general education) map to what students will be expected complete in an assignment or course?
Assessment	Balancing the needs for institutional and program assessment (assessment *of* learning) with individual self-assessment and personal development (assessment *for* learning) is critical for students who are quick to judge and dismiss the value of ePortfolios, particularly if they feel it is busy work or just another requirement to check off. How can ePortfolios be personally meaningful and support the self-assessment needs of students as they make decisions about majors, careers, and personal pursuits?
ePortfolio Tools and Technologies	Recognizing that the institutional learning ePortfolio must compete with commercial web sites in their usability, look, and feel, can students create a professional online presence using the institution's ePortfolio tool? What resources are available to support students in ePortfolio creation and maintenance?
Evaluation of Impact	What would constitute evidence of the positive impact of ePortfolios for students? Some ideas might include the number of student ePortfolios created, student advocacy for ePortfolios on campus, and specific examples of creative and comprehensive student ePortfolios that provide insights into not only *what* students are learning but also *how* and *where* they are learning.

importance of linking reflections with evidence has been a useful exercise that has resulted in reflections characterized by greater depth and explanation of design experiences and has inspired more care and awareness on the part of the teaching team to design reflective prompts and provocative questions in order to elicit more complete and meaningful responses from the students.

Important Considerations

- Think about ways to address potential concerns about the value of ePortfolios that might be raised by learners in your context. Identifying these concerns early on will allow you to manage them during the implementation process.
- Situate your ePortfolio initiative within the broader context of the learning career at your institution and identify milestones in the student pathway as places to introduce and integrate ePortfolio work.
- Develop a "proof-of-concept" opportunity to engage learners in the process. This allows for the development of student examples and "champions"—learners who can model the process for their peers and act as advocates for ePortfolios on your campus.
- Plan to model the process of folio thinking so that learners have opportunities to develop, practice, and receive feedback on this important skill.

5

ePortfolios Outside the Classroom: Involving Campus Partners

For faculty looking to implement ePortfolios in the classroom, it is important to consider the broader range of stakeholders on campus as potential partners. At many institutions, organizations within the wider student affairs umbrella bring a more holistic perspective to student learning and an emphasis on personal and social development and well-being as students develop their identities both inside and outside of the classroom. The use of ePortfolios provides a means to integrate these various learning experiences by encouraging learners to make connections between the learning that happens in workplace and community contexts with what occurs in the classroom. These contexts provide many opportunities for students to develop and document their skills and abilities across a wide range of learning outcomes.

Many institutions have adopted some version of the essential learning outcomes identified by the Association of American Colleges and Universities' Liberal Education and Americas' Promise (LEAP) initiative. In a 2010 survey of employers conducted for AAC&U by Hart Research Associates (2010), the majority of those surveyed expressed wanting colleges to "place more emphasis" on essential learning outcomes including written and oral communication (89%); teamwork skills in diverse groups (71%); creativity and innovation (70%); and civic knowledge, participation, and engagement (52%). Obviously, evidence of how these learning outcomes are met is not limited to the academic work that happens in the classroom. Informal learning experiences through co-ops and internships, residence halls, jobs, and involvement in student activities and community service also foster and contribute to the development of skills related to these learning outcomes.

Documenting these extra-curricular and co-curricular experiences within the academic framework is a key outcome of introducing ePortfolios and a culture of folio thinking. These kinds of experiences can often be quite significant and meaningful to students but are perceived as completely separate from formal academic work. Not only can an ePortfolio provide a context for integration of all learning as it occurs both inside and outside the classroom, but it can also make visible the internships, jobs, study abroad, and work in the community that are often opaque to faculty instructors. At the same time, it is important to note that the person who is in the best position to make the connections between formal and informal learning experiences is the student, thereby emphasizing once again the role of the ePortfolio in encouraging ownership of one's learning and intellectual development.

This ownership is important for two reasons: (1) the reflective process of developing an ePortfolio can increase the individual's personal awareness and self-understanding of his or her intellectual growth; and (2) the ePortfolio product is useful as a concrete context to facilitate conversations with external audiences and to communicate a richer and more representative story of "who I am." The folio thinking approach emphasizes formative assessment during the process of portfolio creation. In other words, the artifacts within the ePortfolio are recognized as tangible points of entry into conversations that might otherwise be too abstract to be effective. These representations of experiences in the ePortfolio that are immediate in the students' minds help facilitate their conversations with others, while having these artifacts handy allow the students to connect and communicate their thoughts in ways other than using words alone.

Of course, students often do not know that they ought to be making these connections or, if they are aware of the benefits of doing so, they are unsure whether it is acceptable to do so, particularly in an academic context. For this reason, it is important for faculty instructors who are initiating ePortfolio work to make explicit the benefits of doing so (see Chapter Four) but also to increase awareness of the co-curricular learning that is being undertaken by their learners at their institution so that they can help them to make those important connections.

The concept of a Learning Landscape introduced in Chapter One highlights how the ePortfolio can facilitate the documentation of the various ways that learners can transfer the knowledge and skills gained in one context to another. This integration does not occur naturally (National Research Council, 2000) and ePortfolios can help scaffold and support this process for learners by engaging external partners to facilitate this knowledge transfer and deep learning. This chapter explores some of the ways that student affairs practitioners and other external partners can be actively included in campus ePortfolio initiatives. Specifically, we focus on ways to promote civic engagement, capitalize on employment opportunities for learners, and document co-curricular learning on student transcripts. In each of these examples we provide suggestions for ways to connect with campus partners in order to move your ePortfolio initiative forward in an integrated way.

FOSTERING CIVIC ENGAGEMENT

In our rapidly changing world, one of the essential learning outcomes is the ability to develop personal and social responsibility, which is "anchored through active involvement with diverse communities and real-world challenges" (National Leadership Council for Liberal Education and America's Promise, 2007). As such, many programs and organizations on campuses that operate within student affairs are increasingly focused on ways to promote civic engagement among graduates. Of course, faculty instructors are also interested in developing these skills and abilities among their learners. The ePortfolio can provide a rich space through which to facilitate the ability of learners to make connections between and among these opportunities. For faculty instructors, it may be useful to survey campus partners to discover what relevant activities are happening on campus with respect to documenting learning in order to identify possible partnerships or shared activities that could be integrated into your course or program.

One example of a campuswide initiative is at the Center for Service and Learning at Indiana University Purdue University Indianapolis (IUPUI), which has conducted a series of pilot projects to actively explore ways in which ePortfolios can support student documentation of their civic learning and development of a sense of civic purpose. These projects have allowed researchers, faculty, and staff to capture and measure the impact of co-curricular activities as well as assist in strengthening student civic learning outcomes. Norris, Price, and Steinberg

(2011) have developed a working definition of a "civic learning pathway" described as:

A threaded set of community-engaged learning experiences in which students, through structured critical reflection:

- articulate their developing understanding of themselves, their relationships and commitments as members of communities, and
- progressively demonstrate their ability to integrate civic knowledge, skills and dispositions as part of their framework for acting in the world.

In the developmental civic learning pathway, ePortfolios are used to guide students as they set goals, engage in academically meaningful service, chart their learning growth and skills development over time, as well as present themselves virtually to others who share an interest in service and civic engagement. Students use an ePortfolio to document, represent, and store their collection of civic learning–related artifacts. The ePortfolio-based civic learning pathway is also designed to enable faculty and other evaluators to access, review, and map authentic artifacts that represent a student's learning relative to specific civic learning outcomes as well as institutional level outcomes.

Michelle Donaldson was interested in building on her experience with community service–learning and the course outcomes allowed her to bring in past experiences as well as look for future opportunities to develop these skills. See http://eport.uwaterloo.ca/html/snapshot.php?id=45894399886853.

For faculty instructors, the ability to engage learners around specific outcomes that might also match goals of other programs is often an important way to develop partnerships and engage learners in making connections between learning contexts. At St. Jerome's University at the University of Waterloo, first-year students have the opportunity to take a transition course called "Reflection and Action" that engages them in dialogue around core texts while also helping them to develop the skills necessary to be successful students and to be responsible citizens. Other campus partners also share similar goals including St. Jerome's Centre for Responsible Citizenship that offers a Beyond Borders community service–learning program. Though the course is offered in the academic context and is not explicitly connected to Beyond Borders, efforts are made to provide opportunities for students to develop their sense of themselves as responsible citizens while introducing them to the Beyond Borders program as an opportunity to pursue in their upper years. This approach, which works to ensure that students develop the ability to document their learning, make connections, and learn about programming offered by campus partners, is one way to meet the institutional goal of developing personal and social responsibility.

As mentioned in Chapter Three, Virginia Tech's residence life program is aimed at promoting civic engagement. The SERVE (Students Engaging and Responding through Volunteer Experiences) program engages first-year students by situating them in a living-learning environment that aims to foster personal and civic growth. Students study community development and social change theory and then apply that theory in various community service experiences such as those found in local hunger relief agencies. For faculty instructors teaching first-year students outside of this program, ePortfolios present an opportunity to allow students to document their learning and to use evidence from their community experiences to demonstrate how they have met civic engagement and personal responsibility learning outcomes. Faculty members interested in similar issues can also explore partnering with housing and residence life offices as a strategy to expand the opportunities for students to meet course outcomes using evidence from co-curricular experiences and contexts.

ENGAGING EMPLOYERS AND CAREER DEVELOPMENT CENTERS

A key motivation for students to document their learning in ePortfolios is the idea that they could use the ePortfolio to showcase their achievements as part of the application process for a future job or internship. Although students may be focused specifically on the outcome and the product, as educators we also see value in the *process* of creating an ePortfolio, reflecting upon one's experiences, and gaining a deeper understanding of one's own skills and achievements—all of which can be especially useful in the job interview or in writing a cover letter. Having engaged in this process, the student can more quickly articulate his or her strengths and weaknesses, thereby demonstrating both self-assessment and metacognitive skills about learning. Students often question whether employers will actually review ePortfolios. While the traditional résumé is still the standard point of entry into the application process, as an applicant moves through the interview process a thoughtfully designed and insightful profile in an ePortfolio can be useful, particularly when employers are trying to make a decision among a handful of top candidates.

For faculty and instructors, it may be useful to engage employers as reviewers of student ePortfolios, particularly in professional fields or vocational fields. Their involvement can serve multiple purposes. For the students, employers lend some credibility and external validity to coursework and the relevance of what is being learned in the classroom to the profession and their future careers. At the same time, this is an opportunity for employers to see firsthand the preparation of students and perhaps offer some feedback and guidance. For faculty and instructors, interested employers could play a role in both motivating students and perhaps providing feedback on individual ePortfolios thereby expanding the pool of ePortfolio reviewers while also offering opportunities for networking and interaction focused on actual student work.

In Foothill College's Dental Hygiene Program, each student ePortfolio carries the professional "brand" of the institution as well as the program. These ePortfolios have a common look and feel and navigation menu as seen in the template shown in Figure 5.1 and the categories down the left-hand side of the page. The program competencies are defined by the profession's accreditation body and the students who earn their associate's degree in this program qualify to take their National Board and State Licensing exam.

Though ePortfolios have been used successfully as a tool for assessing student as well as evaluating the Foothill's dental hygiene program, it is the feedback from dental offices that employ the program's graduates that validates the importance and the benefits of the ePortfolio approach. These ePortfolios highlight the program's excellent reputation as well as the technological capabilities of the students who are applying for positions. The emphasis on skill sets results in less wordy explanations by program graduates particularly in interviews. The ePortfolio process differentiates these applicants from other candidates, particularly in how these students can succinctly speak to their experiences and clearly articulate what they have learned.

In addition to engaging prospective employers, alumni and members of the community can also play a similar role in reviewing ePortfolios, providing feedback to students, and lending some external credibility and validation of the

Figure 5.1   Foothill College's Dental Hygiene Program ePortfolio

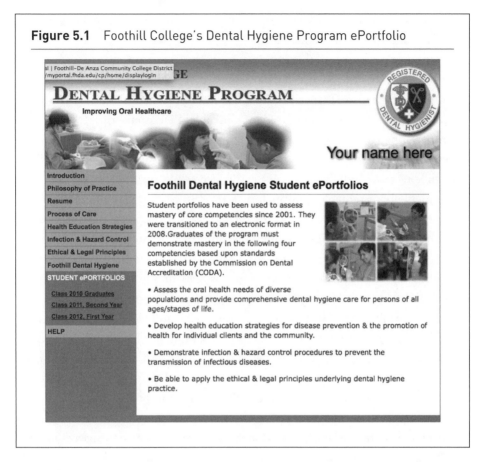

ePortfolio effort. Given that these are digital portfolios, alumni who may not be geographically close but are still interested in engaging with students can also contribute and play a supporting role in alleviating some of the workload involved with giving authentic feedback to students.

ePortfolio as the Official Record? Stanford University's Office of the Registrar's Enhanced Electronic Transcript

Beyond being able to articulate what they have learned, students often want or need verifiable evidence of their achievements and abilities. Though campus registrars do not immediately come to mind as ePortfolio partners and stakeholders, their role as the stewards of student records is critical, particularly as we explore changes in how one's education might be more richly represented from the perspective of the learner and not just the institution.

An interesting example of this exploration is happening at Stanford University where the Office of the Registrar has proposed the concept of an "enhanced electronic transcript" (eTrancript). The eTranscript expands the features and functions of an ePortfolio as a secure, linkable PDF transcript focused on student learning and achievement (Kallman and Nguyen, 2011). This enhanced transcript broadens the functions of accountability, portability, and sustainability of a student record such that it is easily accessible, practically useful, and environmentally sustainable over the long term.

Some of the most exciting features related to this proposed eTranscript as applied to ePortfolios include the ability to embed hyperlinks to actual student artifacts such as a dissertation, a research report, or honors thesis. The criteria for grading can also be included through links to online course descriptions or syllabi. The concept of the eTranscript is predicated upon partnerships with other campus stakeholders including the libraries who archive undergraduate and doctoral theses, course bulletins, and faculty CVs; undergraduate advising; career development services; and centers for teaching and learning. The eTranscript expands the options and uses of transcripts beyond a mere document that students pick up upon graduation on their way out of the university. An eTranscript that is interactive and more frequently accessed encourages students to consider how they want their educational experiences represented in the official record and also what kinds of learning might be missing from their education as they progress through the institution. The application of the ePortfolio model to the traditional transcript has the potential to transform what constitutes meaningful evidence of learning in higher education. This has important implications for faculty instructors who are traditionally responsible for determining whether a student has met the necessary outcomes for graduation. Close partnerships with campus stakeholders who are also interested in ePortfolios for a variety of purposes will make the initiative more effective, efficient, scalable, and sustainable.

These examples of campus partnerships are meant to provide a sense of the possibilities for faculty members in terms of other stakeholders who might be interested in ePortfolio work. As with other aspects of designing an effective

Table 5.1 Implications for Using ePortfolios with Campus Partners

Implementation Step	Guiding Questions
Learning Outcomes	Given the learning outcomes for your course or program, are there other campus groups, such as clubs or community service organizations, who might be exploring similar outcomes, e.g., civic engagement, personal and social responsibility, etc.?
Stakeholders	Think "outside the box." Who are other possible partners on campus and off campus who share your interests and goals and can benefit from and contribute to an ePortfolio effort? How will engaging these partners help learners to integrate experiences across various learning contexts (in other words, what value will these partners bring to students' efforts to document their learning)?
Learning Activities	Students are deeply interested in the relevance of their classroom work to the "real world." How can the ePortfolio serve as a means for capturing the connections they make in ways that may be unexpected, fleeting, and not readily apparent?
Assessment	Assessment efforts within student affairs and across campus can often be minimal and constrained. How can the ePortfolio capture insights and connections that are not only useful to you as the instructor but also informative for campus partners and their daily work?
ePortfolio Tools and Technologies	Often, students may feel great passion and dedication for their extracurricular activities and their engagement may take the form of digital stories, multimedia websites and promotional materials. How can ePortfolios support the personalization of these experiences, facilitate creativity, and provide a robust platform for archiving and storage?
Evaluation of Impact	Evidence of impact can be captured in descriptions of who is actively involved with the ePortfolio effort, the number of individuals who the student has interacted with, and the new insights that may be revealed for partner organizations via student ePortfolios. How can changes in student perceptions of the relevance of their classroom work and diversity in the kinds of experiences cited as evidence of learning outcomes be explored?

ePortfolio implementation, it is important to consider the outcomes that the ePortfolio is designed to help students meet. This look at possible campus partners, though, highlights the importance of thinking about documenting learning in a holistic way that allows learners to make connections to learning experiences across a variety of contexts.

Important Considerations

- Consider your learning outcomes. Who else on your campus might be interested in having students achieve similar goals? Check out your institution's strategic plan and mission statement as a starting point for understanding what is most valued in your graduates.
- Ask around. Don't assume that you are working alone on an island. Even if there are not others on your campus currently interested in or thinking about ePortfolios, you can find resources and collaborators in the broader ePortfolio community.
- Start a conversation. Engaging potential campus partners in a dialogue around documenting learning is a great way to move ideas forward!

6

Using ePortfolios to Support Assessment

As noted in the Preface, ePortfolios are but one approach in a suite of assessment tools that aim to gather evidence of student progress and development in learning outcomes identified at the individual course, program, or institutional level (Leskes and Wright, 2005; Leskes and Miller, 2006). As discussed in the previous chapters, defining learning outcomes is the necessary first step in identifying how and where ePortfolios can facilitate and support assessment efforts. Given that only 4% of AAC&U member institutions surveyed in 2009 were *not* considering the use of ePortfolios for assessment (over three-quarters of the 433 institutional respondents reported having a common set of intended learning outcomes for undergraduates and 96% are either currently assessing or planning for assessment of learning outcomes across the curriculum), it is clear that defining intended learning outcomes and establishing a means to assess whether they are being met represent an important and prevalent trend (Hart Research Associates, 2009).

Once these outcomes are established, a useful exercise is described by Kelly (2010) in Figure 6.1, who maps AAC&U's essential learning outcomes (introduced in Chapter One) to institutional, college, department, or program goals and further to the individual course objectives, down to the specific assignment that guides students in producing the artifact that would be considered evidence of how the learning outcome is met. This mapping activity encourages ePortfolio stakeholders to think carefully about how learning outcomes, particularly at

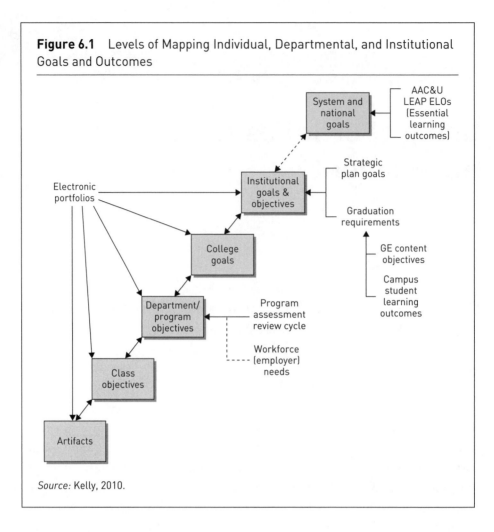

Figure 6.1 Levels of Mapping Individual, Departmental, and Institutional Goals and Outcomes

Source: Kelly, 2010.

the institutional level, are operationalized into actual assignments that students would understand. It is also a very challenging activity as it requires stakeholders to struggle with definitions (e.g., "what is critical thinking?"), measures (e.g., "what tools or metrics could I use to determine whether a student has improved their critical thinking skills?"), and most important, evidence (e.g., "what artifacts or work products with accompanying reflections could students produce to demonstrate their competency in critical thinking?").

This mapping suggests the ways that ePortfolio technology can contribute to the assessment of individual students and learning outcomes at the course, department, program, and institutional levels. This chapter provides an overview of this process which, when combined with a culture of reflection and folio thinking, can provide advantages over traditional assessment approaches, such as standardized exams.

ASSESSMENT *OF* LEARNING VERSUS ASSESSMENT *FOR* LEARNING

Once the learning outcomes have been defined, it would be useful to consider the goals for using ePortfolios as an assessment tool and what insights into student learning an ePortfolio approach can effectively provide. A useful characterization that Dr. Helen Barrett, a pioneer and leader in the field of ePortfolios, has actively explored is the distinction between assessment *of* learning versus assessment *for* learning, as described in Table 6.1 (Barrett, 2004).

Program evaluation and institutional accreditation activities that are mandated by external bodies or senior administration, where faculty and students are expected to follow some kind of standardized template or reporting guidelines, typically fall under the assessment *of* learning column. In many ways, these ePortfolios function more like an assessment management system in this context, simply providing a framework for the uploading, organization, and accessing of artifacts. Additional features might include facilitating the evaluation of sampled

Table 6.1 Assessment *of* Learning Versus Assessment *for* Learning

Assessment *of* learning	Assessment *for* learning
Purpose prescribed	Purpose negotiated
Artifacts mandated and scored for external use	Artifacts chosen by learner and feedback provided back to learner
Organized by the instructor/teacher	Organized by the learner
Summative (past to present)	Formative (present to future)
Institution-centered	Student-centered
Requires extrinsic motivation	Intrinsically motivating
Positivist	Constructivist

artifacts by allowing individual evaluators to easily access rubrics and artifacts and submit their reports electronically. Reporting functions summarizing these reviews can then be generated for outside evaluators and program reviews.

In contrast, most of the interest in learning ePortfolios and the benefits that are usually touted for students fall under the assessment *for* learning column. This more holistic and longer-term perspective emphasizes student ownership of a learning career that is driven by the interests, passions, and goals of the individual learner. As a result, the ePortfolio here is more formative in nature, creative, and personalized with the ability to include both formal and informal aspects of an individual's education. This ePortfolio is more intrinsically motivating for students since they recognize how the folio thinking process and product are focused on their specific interests and not the institution's. At the same time, faculty and administrators can also gain insights into the learning experiences that are afforded by the educational environment based on what students decide is worth documenting in their ePortfolios.

The dichotomy of an institutionally mandated checklist of competencies aimed to address accreditation concerns versus a reflective personal digital story created by a student to support his or her own growth and development naturally raises the question of whether ePortfolio assessment has to be one or the other. Dr. Darren Cambridge (2010), co-leader of the Inter/National Coalition for Electronic Portfolio Research, questions this depiction of extremes and characterizes assessment *of* learning as ePortfolios designed to assess *for* institutional, not individual, learning. This issue relates back to the mapping exercise described by Kelly (2010) and how ePortfolios can support student self-assessment but also inform and contribute to institutional improvement and educational effectiveness, involving all campus stakeholders ranging from senior leadership to individual students.

USE OF RUBRICS IN ePORTFOLIO ASSESSMENT

The use of rubrics in ePortfolio assessment, particularly at the program and institutional level, has emerged due to concerns about the qualitative nature of ePortfolios and issues of reliability, particularly when compared to the quantitative results of standardized tests. The Valid Assessment of Learning in Undergraduate Education (VALUE) project of the Association of American Colleges and

Universities began to address these questions by developing rubrics for each of the essential learning outcomes described in the Liberal Education America's Promise (LEAP) initiative. The goals of the VALUE project were to: (1) assess learning over time; (2) share expectations and rubrics that describe achievement levels; and (3) develop ePortfolios as tools for learning and assessment. VALUE project leaders Terrel Rhodes and Wende Garrison provide training workshops where raters collectively review examples of student work and practice applying the rubrics for the purpose of calibrating and norming the raters' understanding of what the rubrics mean to ensure that the raters reach the same conclusions about a student's achievement of a particular learning outcome. This process results in more reliable results, a higher correlation and lower discrepancies between raters.

These rubrics are a useful starting point not only for defining the desired characteristics of, for example, critical thinking or teamwork, but also for describing what kinds of evidence would demonstrate competency in these areas. Although rubrics can obviously be used independently of ePortfolios, the application of rubrics for assessing multimedia examples of student work collected via ePortfolios is currently being explored. In addition, a well-designed rubric that represents the criteria and standards as defined by the institution can also serve to communicate these expectations for success to the students themselves (see http://www.aacu.org/value/rubrics/pdf/CriticalThinking.pdf for an example). The rubrics become roadmaps for students to use to navigate and understand where they should be when they graduate from the institution (i.e., what skills they should have acquired through their educational experiences) and ideally, what resources and supports are available to help them get there (Rhodes, 2010).

Student self-assessment using ePortfolios is one significant benefit of this approach because the artifacts submitted to the instructor also remain visible and accessible to the student. As a result, this continuing access to the electronic artifacts within the ePortfolio makes it possible to partner with students in the assessment process. Students are asked to share what they think constitutes evidence of what they are learning and how they are fulfilling the institutionally defined educational objectives. The conclusions they come to are not only evident to the institution but also remain visible to themselves through their ePortfolios.

The following two examples demonstrate how ePortfolios have been successfully used to assess learning outcomes at the individual and course levels and at the program and institutional levels. Both approaches follow a similar process as described in the ePortfolio implementation framework.

Assessing Experiential Education Competencies in the Culinary Arts at Johnson & Wales University

As a career-focused teaching institution, Johnson & Wales University (JWU)—a regionally accredited private not-for-profit institution with campuses in Providence, Rhode Island; North Miami, Florida; Denver, Colorado; and Charlotte, North Carolina—has a decade of experience using portfolios for career planning and student professional development in undergraduate programs of study. In recent years the university suspended use of its traditional paper portfolio and is exploring the use of ePortfolios instead. The transition to ePortfolios is aligned with a shift to outcomes-based assessment, moving from an employer orientation (portfolio as career tool) to a student focus (portfolio as a platform for student learning), from artifact collection to critical reflection, and toward an ePortfolio that emphasizes assessment to ensure student learning rather than career marketing.

JWU has defined a set of experiential education competencies that include disciplinary knowledge and skills such as professionalism, problem solving, communication, and collaboration. Although JWU is still in the early stages of their ePortfolio initiative, Maureen Dumas, vice president of Experiential Education and Career Services, states that the institution has given much thought to how student reflection in experiential education can support learning and development. Guiding this development is JWU's *InCoRe* model which focuses on the "strategic *integration* of experiential education within a program of study, the *coordination* of student advising between faculty and the administrators and staff members who manage and support experiential education and student-based *reflection* oriented toward fulfillment of student learning outcomes" (Griffin, Lorenz, and Mitchell, 2011, 42).

Regular reflection is scaffolded through a skills journal designed to help students document and monitor the skills they develop throughout their internship by assessing and reflecting upon their experiences, learning opportunities, strengths, and weaknesses relative to the experiential education competencies. The skills journals are submitted on a biweekly basis and graded on the quality of information submitted, spelling, grammar, and tone as they relate to the experiential education competencies. Building on Kiser's integrative processing model (1998), JWU developed the following framework to guide students through the critical reflective process of their internship experiences:

Early Reflection (Week 2): Consider your internship experience over the first few weeks:
- What have you observed about your internship experience so far?
- How will you be effective in your internship? Review the general workplace skills and behaviors: professionalism and work ethic, problem solving, communications, collaboration, disciplinary knowledge and skills. What goals do you have in developing these skills?

Real-Time Reflection (Week 6): Consider your existing academic and practical knowledge and answer the following questions:
- How is the internship experience consistent with your academic knowledge and coursework?
- How did your knowledge gained from your coursework help you organize, understand, and make sense of the internship experience?
- How does your internship experience contradict or challenge the knowledge you gained from your coursework?

Reflection and Next Steps (Week 9): Consider your overall internship experience.
- What were the key events or highlights of your internship experience?
- Consider the question: "Where do I go from here with my work, career, and learning?"
- Submit an updated version of your résumé which includes the various skills and experiences gained.

It should be noted that JWU's use of skills journals and the emphasis on reflection has established a culture that is receptive to exploring how ePortfolios can enhance these practices that are already in place. The culture encompasses more than just the culinary arts and has grown to include the college of business and other programs on campus. Instead of e-mailing the skills journals to their experiential education coordinators, students can upload them to an ePortfolio that they can continue to access and their supervisors can regularly monitor. This incorporation of ePortfolios will build upon JWU's proposed hypothesis that regular intervals of student-based reflection will enhance student learning from their internship experiences by facilitating the documentation of evidence toward the assessment of institutional level experiential education outcomes.

Course-Level ePortfolio Assessment in Engineering Technology

The use of ePortfolios to assess students at the individual course level has been explored by the University of Delaware's undergraduate engineering technology program which has taken the standards of their accrediting body, ABET, and translated them into workplace competencies for a first-year seminar course. Examples of these workplace competencies include integrity, communication, cultural adaptability, innovation, and teamwork. Using the Situation Task Action Result (STAR) approach developed by Brumm, Mickelson, and White (2006) at Iowa State University, students in the first-year seminar demonstrate in their first semester how they have met two of the fourteen workplace competencies—Engineering/Technical Knowledge and Planning—by uploading into their ePortfolio either (1) an artifact of their choosing or (2) a completed STAR form. Students using the STAR form are introduced to reflection that is outlined in a problem-solving action step approach:

- *Situation:* Give an example of a situation you were involved in that resulted in a positive outcome.
- *Task:* Describe the tasks involved in that situation.
- *Action:* What were the various actions involved in the situation's task?
- *Results:* What results directly followed because of your actions?

Each of these ePortfolio postings is accompanied by a reflection for each competency, prompted by the following questions:

- To what degree have you achieved the competency?
- How does the attached artifact or STAR show that you have demonstrated the key actions for the competency?

- What have you learned as you've developed and demonstrated the competency?

- What will you do differently or continue to do as a result of the experiences documented by the artifacts or STARs?

Using an interactive evaluation form to provide formative feedback on student work, both faculty and students can see the scores they receive and the impact of the scores on their grades. Two of the criteria for evaluating either the ePortfolio artifacts or completed STAR forms are similar to what is used by JWU in their focus on how both the artifacts and accompanying reflections demonstrate how the competencies have been met. The use of the STAR forms embedded in multiple courses is part of a programwide assessment effort aimed at providing formative feedback to students and to the department through the aggregation of data from individual courses which can, in turn, inform programmatic improvement and the engineering ABET accreditation process.

Both of these examples illustrate how ePortfolios can enhance existing practices and ongoing assessment efforts by streamlining and facilitating the aggregation of student- and course-level assessment data to inform outcomes at the program and department levels. The use of reflective prompts reiterates the observations of Nancy Wozniak of SUNY Stony Brook who found that "Students reflect naturally, but don't seem to apply it for producing evidence of learning in their ePortfolio. I found I needed to promote the use of prompts with the students starting out with 'folio thinking' and the academic level didn't matter, including the graduate level. I found that the students that continued to work on their ePortfolios and include self-directed activities in other courses and areas of their lives were able to reflect without prompts. They had to grow into folio thinking and reflection." In assessing students' development of folio thinking skills, promoting a longitudinal perspective of tracking students over time through their academic years and into their professional careers could be quite fruitful and revealing. Student learning ePortfolios in particular can further engage learners in the assessment process with more frequent formative feedback and regular reflection compiled in an ePortfolio that makes their learning more visible to others as well as themselves.

Table 6.2 Implications for Using ePortfolios to Support Assessment

Implementation Step	Guiding Questions
Learning Outcomes	How are you defining the learning outcomes for your students, course, department, program, or institution? This is a critical step that is necessary in order to guide the planning of an ePortfolio assessment effort.
Stakeholders	Identifying the stakeholders in an assessment effort can influence how ePortfolios will be used and what kinds of data and evidence will be gathered, particularly for broader assessments at the program, department, or institutional levels. Who is interested in seeing what information is collected?
Learning Activities	How are institutional- and program-level learning outcomes operationalized into actual activities and assignments that students will complete and upload into their ePortfolios? How can reflection and self-assessment be scaffolded to support these activities?
Assessment	How will the artifacts that are produced for the ePortfolio be evaluated? How can rubrics be designed and used to accurately represent the learning outcomes and effectively communicate their meaning to students as well as external evaluators?
ePortfolio Tools and Technologies	How can the features of the ePortfolio support and automate some of the reporting functions by aggregating and streamlining data to provide formative feedback to students and to inform programmatic decisions?
Evaluation of Impact	How can reflections in combination with ePortfolio creation generate new insights into student learning that would otherwise be invisible and difficult to document using traditional assessment approaches?

Important Considerations

- Consider your learning outcomes and think about how you will assess ePortfolios and how your assessment efforts might map to other contexts (course → program → institution).
- Think about how you might partner with students in your assessment activities. Instead of assessment being something that is done "to" them, how might students assist and inform the design of reflective prompts and the organization of evidence through their ePortfolios?
- Develop and adapt rubrics for assessment that will communicate clearly *what* is being assessed and *how* that will be done (that is, which artifacts will represent clear evidence of learning to the various stakeholders).

PART 3

Practical Considerations for Implementing ePortfolios

art Three focuses on practical considerations for implementing ePortfolios. We explore faculty development issues, technology solutions and resources, and ways to evaluate the impact of the ePortfolio initiative for documenting learning.

7

Faculty Development and ePortfolios

In Chapters Two and Three, we outlined the implementation framework used to think through the design of effective and efficient ePortfolio projects to document learning. This framework is useful for understanding the issues related to instructional design and to stakeholders' needs when using ePortfolios. It can also be used to create effective faculty development programming in order to engage faculty instructors in the process of redesigning their course or program to include ePortfolios. When considering this framework for documenting learning, it is especially important for instructors to clearly articulate the learning outcomes that they wish to achieve. Despite the fact that many new technologies are available for incorporation into courses and programs to engage students, the most important thing to consider when experimenting with a new approach is the pedagogical affordances that the technology might provide. In other words, it is important to ensure that the pedagogy leads the technology use, and not the other way around.

For faculty instructors, approaching the design or redesign of a course through a focus on pedagogy is sometimes not as intuitive as might be assumed. Often, instructors teach the way they themselves were taught. Though these approaches often do work without requiring significant modifications, experimenting with a new approach like ePortfolios can significantly alter the effectiveness of tried-and-true methods, because instructors will need to align teaching, learning, and assessment methods with the learning outcomes that are to be achieved. Thinking carefully about how the ePortfolio can contribute to significant and meaningful learning for students can ensure the success of the initiative. It can also help minimize the time required to implement a new approach, which is certainly one of the chief concerns that faculty instructors have when they are asked to try something different in the classroom (either online, face-to-face, or in a hybrid setting). Effective faculty development programming can also ensure that faculty who are being asked to implement ePortfolios (including those who are "early adopters") can feel supported in their efforts and limit the risks that may accompany a new approach (such as lower student evaluation scores).

Many institutions have implemented programming to support the use of ePortfolios that suits the culture of their particular setting. This chapter explores some of the key issues that can be addressed by effective faculty development programming. First is the need to situate the goal of documenting learning within the existing campus culture. Helping faculty to understand how ePortfolios fit with what they already do can alleviate instructor trepidation about using ePortfolios. Second, we outline ways to deal with buy-in, training, and support for the use of ePortfolios. Finally, we consider how to evaluate campus culture and readiness for an ePortfolio implementation and suggest ways to design an intervention that fits your institution's cultural context. These issues are important in determining the appropriate intervention for a particular campus culture that will engage faculty in ePortfolio activities around learning outcomes and set instructors up for success by providing resources to allow them to implement ePortfolios in a meaningful way.

UNDERSTANDING THE CAMPUS CULTURE AND ASSESSING WHERE ePORTFOLIOS WORK

There are many ways to encourage faculty instructors to undertake ePortfolio work. It is important to consider the culture on a particular campus to ensure that the way the ePortfolio is introduced fits with that particular context. In many regards, this consideration must go back to the issue of stakeholders—who are they on your campus and what particular approach speaks to their needs? It is also important to consider the overall landscape of the institution to determine where ePortfolio opportunities might already exist. For instance, campus strategic plans and mission statements can provide insights into what is valued at an institution, and what the goals for the future are. For instance, at the University of Waterloo, the sixth decade plan (http://www.sixthdecade.uwaterloo.ca/) highlights the goals that the university will focus on in a ten-year period. ePortfolio work can be mapped to those goals to ensure that the documentation of learning supports the achievement of those aspirations.

For faculty instructors, though, this process of considering stakeholders and the campus culture is not something that is necessarily intuitive. Often, we design our courses with our disciplines in mind, and perhaps even with departmental or programmatic goals as a focus, but we do not have a sense of the wider campus ethos in which we are operating. As such, an innovation like ePortfolios may not initially be connected to the needs or goals of the campus culture. Yet documenting learning is inherently bigger than an individual course because the approach, by its nature, asks learners to make connections between their varied learning experiences. Faculty development programming which pays close attention to the wider campus culture and needs of stakeholders can ensure that faculty instructors are set up for success in their ePortfolio implementation.

Buy-In, Training, and Support for ePortfolios

Encouraging faculty to incorporate ePortfolios into their current practice is often met with trepidation because it can call into question current practices. Many instructors feel threatened by the increase in transparency brought on by the formal documentation of learning in something like an ePortfolio. This is not an uncommon experience at any institution seeking to implement an approach that makes the learning that happens in a classroom (either online or face-to-face) more visible. One of the keys to obtaining buy-in from faculty instructors for the adoption of a new approach like ePortfolios is to highlight the ways that the new method aligns with current practice. For instance, rather than asking instructors to transform their course, find out what they are already doing and discuss how the ePortfolio can help them to be more successful or how it can help them to meet an outcome that is challenging for learners. When having these conversations, it is important to talk about ePortfolio learning in a way that is meaningful to the particular discipline. For instance, in engineering, it might not make sense to talk about learners "reflecting" on their learning or adopting a folio thinking approach. The response might be that reflection is not part of the curriculum. Yet, engineers do create design documents, which outline the rationale for design decisions in a project. A design rationale document is inherently reflective as it looks back on decisions and documents them, yet they are not referred to as reflections per se. In this example, knowledge of the approaches, language, and methods employed in a disciplinary context can inform ways to communicate the benefits of ePortfolios that speak to the needs of the stakeholders (in this case, the faculty member and the students).

Once buy-in has been established, it is important to develop training that assists the faculty instructor to use ePortfolios to meet existing outcomes or to address those that tackle wider departmental, programmatic, or institutional goals. In addition to training, consider the types of support that will be required in order to ensure that the implementation is successful. This might include support for the faculty instructor in a given course, and also for students using ePortfolios or other stakeholders interested in the initiative (for instance, other campus partners who want to use ePortfolio artifacts in their own work).

It should be remembered that using ePortfolios and similar approaches to document student learning does not need to diminish academic freedom, nor should it be viewed as oppressive. Most often it represents authentic evidence of the exceptional work of faculty. In addition, the formal documentation of learning can provide evidence of connections between work being done in different disciplines and across a campus that point to shared values and goals. This can be very validating and freeing, particularly when this work helps to illuminate campuswide goals. Documentation of these efforts can also highlight areas for improvement, which can ensure that the hard work needed to remedy areas for concern are targeted and timely.

Evaluating Campus Culture: Interventions That "Fit"

It is important to situate appropriate strategies for buy-in, training, and support within the broader campus culture. Each institutional culture is slightly different so consider the various approaches used at different campuses and determine which most closely align with your own. For instance, your culture might be focused on implementing new technologies in teaching and learning and ePortfolios might be one of a set of technologies available for instructors to use. At Virginia Tech (VT), all faculty instructors have the opportunity to upgrade their computers every four years. In order to take advantage of this offer, though, they need to attend Faculty Development Institute (FDI) workshops, which provide training on a number of pedagogical and technological solutions that can be used in the classroom. The ePortfolio Initiatives, based in the Department of Learning Technologies, view the FDI as an opportunity to offer training to faculty on the implementation and use of ePortfolios in their classrooms. As such, they regularly offer a number of ePortfolio workshops within the technology tracks that help to spread the word about ePortfolios as they introduce instructors to the ways that they can be used to make learning meaningful for their students.

Whereas the FDI workshops provide a way to engage faculty with new technologies for teaching and learning, also important to the teaching faculty at VT is the ability to implement a new approach that can increase student engagement. This is often a key driver for instructors in exploring ePortfolios. Initially, most ePortfolio adoption at VT focused on accreditation efforts, with instructors simply using the approach to gather accreditation data, for professional development, or to aid students in creating online résumés (products of learning with little emphasis on the process of reflecting on learning). What they quickly learned was that students were not engaged in this process because they did not understand how this documentation (the act of producing a résumé) was helping them in their own learning. As such, the ePortfolio Initiatives team has developed workshops that address the ways that ePortfolios can help instructors meet the goals, objectives, and learning outcomes of their courses so that the value of ePortfolios can be more effectively communicated to students, while also relating their ePortfolio work to wider accreditation efforts (see Figure 7.1).

The team also addresses issues of concern to faculty like the amount of time needed to incorporate ePortfolios into existing curriculum and dealing with the intimidation that some instructors feel when faced with a new technology for teaching and learning. Their three-pronged approach (see Exhibit 7.1) focuses on assessment, learning environments (educational activities and reflection), and professional development for students (graduate programs or professional résumés, or a focus on ePortfolios as an output rather than a process). Usually, clients come with one of these three needs as the primary focus, but what often happens as the project is developed is that the other two prongs become more significant.

Even when faculty come with a need in mind that is more focused on students developing a product for professional purposes (that is, ePortfolio as résumé or

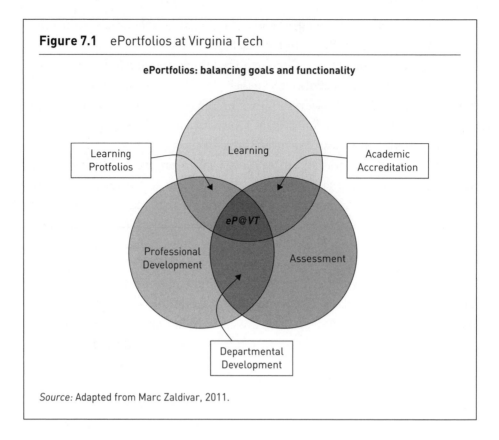

Figure 7.1 ePortfolios at Virginia Tech

ePortfolios: balancing goals and functionality

Learning Protfolios

Academic Accreditation

Learning

eP@VT

Professional Development

Assessment

Departmental Development

Source: Adapted from Marc Zaldivar, 2011.

a product), the ePortfolio Initiative team works with instructors and encourages them to consider how they might incorporate some reflection into the project or how they might collect evidence that can be used for assessment. At VT, blending "pure" assessment with student needs regarding what both students and faculty want to get out of ePortfolio work has really helped faculty make a smoother transition to ePortfolios in the classroom, where engaging students is as equally important as engaging faculty. The FDI workshops (see Exhibit 7.2) are a good way to reach new faculty and get them thinking about how to use ePortfolios in their courses and even programs. These workshops provide an opportunity for the team to make the first contact, which they can then follow up after the workshop in face-to-face meetings with individuals and even whole departments that want to do this type of work. The FDI provides

Exhibit 7.1   Examples of Programs at Virginia Tech That Have Adopted the Three-Pronged Approach

Two examples of programs that have evolved into a three-pronged approach to ePortfolio adoption at Virginia Tech are the Department of English and the Dietetics Program within the Human Nutrition, Food, and Exercise department. In the first case, the English department was motivated to begin examining student learning outcomes by a university initiative focused on assessment. Recognizing the lack of an external organization to provide specific learning outcomes, the first challenge was to define those learning outcomes for the English department. ePortfolios provided a way to collect direct evidence of student work for that assessment, as very little other evidence was used in the department. The first iteration of the English Department ePortfolio was purely assessment oriented, asking students to submit representative work for departmental outcomes into a "checklist" type of system. Within one semester, it became clear that the culture of the program and of the student body would not satisfactorily adopt this approach: there simply was no place for creativity and the personalization needed for these students to represent themselves as individuals. Revising the model, and incorporating an "ePortfolio leadership team" made up of a dozen students, the department rethought the place of learning and professional development spaces within the ePortfolio, working with the ePortfolio Initiatives team to develop a web-based individualized template that allowed for student creativity to take the forefront, while still collecting the representative work needed to assess the department's learning outcomes. Samples of these ePortfolios can be found at http://eportfolio.vt.edu/englishgallery.html.

In the second case, the Dietetics program had a long-standing assessment-oriented portfolio tradition, though it was paper based. The program collected a paper binder that contained ten specific assignments from each graduating student, demonstrating professional competencies as defined by their external professional organization, the Commission on Accreditation for Dietetics Education (CADE). The first iteration of their ePortfolio, then, duplicated this process, again using a checklist approach to collect the same ten assignments in digital format for easier transmission to and review of these materials by their accreditors. However, students were not engaged with the process and, once again, an ePortfolio team was put together consisting of a dozen students interested in evaluating that model. Those students developed two parallel pieces to the ePortfolio. The first was an expanded checklist that, though focused on CADE professional outcomes, provided more variety in the types of assignments that students chose to represent including outcomes such as Professionalism and Ethics or Disciplinary Knowledge. The "Student Assessment Matrix" used language to describe this effort such as, "Students may choose to include . . ." followed by a list of example assignments from various courses in the program, as well as a list of out-of-classroom experiences that could also be documented. The assessment matrix, while used for programmatic assessment, was "sold" to the students as a place for self-assessment for their attainment of the professional standards of the discipline. In addition to this matrix, the student team designed a flexible template that would serve as a place to represent their learning and their professional development, and a second template that could be used to apply for internships that represents a vital step in their professional career. Samples of these portfolios can be found at http://eportfolio.vt.edu/hnfegallery.html.

Taken together, these two approaches demonstrate that students are aware of the value of ePortfolios beyond assessment, even self-assessment. ePortfolios, for students, can serve as a useful place to collect and reflect upon learning, and represent that work in a professional capacity.

a formal mechanism for faculty to consider the use of technology in their classrooms in a way that encourages a focus on learning outcomes and what activities are appropriate to meet those outcomes. It is a way to give instructors an opportunity to begin thinking about redesigning their courses that is designed to set them up for success.

A much different institutional context is that of Western Governor's University (WGU), a fully online university. WGU faces the same challenges as other traditional institutions in obtaining faculty buy-in for new approaches in pedagogy and technology. In the case of ePortfolios, WGU needs to help faculty to understand what formal documentation of student learning is and why it is important for them to transform their traditional course design and overall approach to education to one that begins with the end in mind. One method that WGU has found to be very effective is called an Assessment Sketch. Assessment Sketches could just as easily be called Documentation of Learning Sketches, ePortfolio Sketches, or Show What You Know Sketches, and so on, because this is how they function. Conceptualized by WGU Assessment Development Managers Gerilee Nicastro and Kyle Moreton, Assessment Sketches are templates that provide scaffolded support for academic faculty as they transform their courses and educational practices. The templates assist faculty through the use of guiding questions designed to elicit responses that lead to converting a traditionally designed course into one where student learning outcomes and the associated methods of formal documentation have been identified and planned. Moreover, the Assessment Sketches provide guidance for faculty to ensure that the instructional and learning resources are aligned to the student learning outcomes and associated formal methods of documentation. Core elements of the Assessment Sketches are sections including: 1) demographic information regarding the course; 2) prompts to help faculty identify assumed

Exhibit 7.2   Virginia Tech: Example Workshops for ePortfolio Engagement in the Faculty Development Institute

These three workshops provide faculty instructors with scaffolded ways to engage faculty instructors with ePortfolios. The first is an "overview" workshop, where the goal is to introduce faculty who are new to the concept of using ePortfolios in their approach to assessment, learning, and professional development. The second workshop focuses on demonstrating effective ePortfolio implementation in various programs around campus, allowing faculty to ask specific questions and to consider which parts of the model work for their context. The last workshop is devoted to VT's first-year experience ePortfolio, as this is a campuswide program and eventually will affect all entering students at Virginia Tech. This workshop explains the use of ePortfolios to entering students and discusses the similarities and differences in the approaches used by the different First-Year Experience (FYE) programs. Unlike other institutions, each department or college may decide how to implement the learning goals for the first-year experiences within existing or new courses, rather than having one central course that all students at VT take (for more information about the FYE initiative, see http://www.fye.vt.edu).

Following are course descriptions of each workshop.

1. ePortfolio: Virginia Tech's ePortfolio System Within Scholar (the VT Learning Management and Collaboration System)

Virginia Tech's ePortfolio system is a web-based, interactive tool designed to help students create, organize, reflect on, and share evidence of their educational accomplishments, both in courses and extracurricular activities. The ePortfolio is also seen as a tool to assist programs and departments with self-studies, assessment, and accreditation. This short course explores these and other applications of ePortfolios. The pros and cons of traditional applications of portfolios will be outlined, as will a generalized model of the portfolio process. The changes enabled by ePortfolios will be highlighted and ePortfolio's evolution at Virginia Tech will be discussed. The ePortfolio is quite flexible; however, faculty wishing to use it must make a number of decisions as they design how they would like the system to work. An overview of this design process will be provided along with documentation and other resources that will aid faculty as they move toward an adoption of ePortfolios. An in-depth, hands-on exploration of the latest version of this software will follow the conceptual discussion.

2. ePortfolios Everywhere: Projects at Virginia Tech

ePortfolios are being used across the university for a wide variety of purposes, including learning, assessment, and professional development. The ePortfolio tools within Scholar offer ways to help students create, organize, reflect on, and share evidence of their educational accomplishments, both in courses and extracurricular activities. The tools can also assist programs and departments with self-studies, assessment, and accreditation. This short course presents a range of successful ePortfolio projects from around campus. An in-depth discussion of portfolio development will be provided. Examples of different types of ePortfolios will be highlighted, including projects that focus on reflective learning, departmental and programmatic assessment, and professional development, as well as ePortfolios that blend two or more of these areas. Plenty of time will be given for discussion and participant questions related to individual ePortfolio needs and implementation within participant courses, programs, and departments.

3. First-Year Experience ePortfolios at Virginia Tech

Fall 2010 marked the first pilot year of Virginia Tech's Quality Enhancement Plan (QEP), related to our university-level accreditation through the Southern Association of Colleges and Schools. The QEP focuses on first-year experiences (FYE) and is intended to encourage processes of problem solving, inquiry, and integrative learning among the first-year students, with the goal of making them more aware of the professional opportunities that are available to them at the university. ePortfolios play a critical role in facilitating both the learning and assessment agendas related to deploying a successful campuswide first-year experience. Based in the undergraduate colleges, each first-year experience has core elements, such as the ePortfolio, an online Course of Study Planner, and the Common Book, but can also be tailored to the individual characteristics of that college. This short course provides an overview of the FYE ePortfolio and offers examples of current FYE ePortfolio projects.

prior knowledge of students; 3) specific course outcomes; 4) a space for faculty identify the types of measures to be used to document outcomes; 5) the design plans for each of the measures (see Exhibit 7.3). This approach is an example of how instructors can be supported through the process of implementing ePortfolio activities to facilitate assessment of learning outcomes.

The need to assess learning outcomes is also important at Mercy College in the state of New York. There, the first step in achieving buy-in and support for an ePortfolio initiative began with a small group of faculty who self-organized to explore ePortfolio tools and methods. They took on the identity of a faculty learning community in 2008 after becoming familiar with this model from their research. This community evolved organically into a sustainable ePortfolio program designed to engage students, assess student learning, and promote academic success (https://www.mercy.edu/stafffaculty/fctl/pdf_pamphlets/About_MePort_FLC.pdf). Initially, the learning community explored best practices and selected TaskStream as the technology tool to support the ePortfolio work on the campus. However, three years later, the learning community has grown to over 138 faculty members and is an active space for examples and resources to be shared. It is led by peer faculty leaders who also provide individual

Exhibit 7.3 Assessment Sketch—Western Governors University

Program & Assessment Blueprint Worksheet	
Course Title & CUs	
Program	
Course Code(s)	
Content Areas	What general content areas would be covered in this course? *Course content here*
Course Description	*Course Description Here*
Assumed Prior Knowledge	*Are there any skills or experiences that students must have prior to approaching this assessment? What assumptions are being made about the students at this point in the program?*
Course Outcomes	*Upon successful completion of the course, what would a student be able to demonstrate? Start thinking about the competencies that a student should have mastered in the course and be demonstrating on the assessment. What are the desired outcomes of the course?*
Assessment Type	*What type of assessment might lend itself to these outcomes and expectations?*
Assessment Sketch	*What will the assessment look like? If this is a performance assessment, how many tasks will be included (max = 3 3-level and 1 5-level)? Describe the outcomes desired for each individual task. What will the artifact(s) look like?*

Source: Kyle Mallory Moreton and Geri Nicastro

consultations with colleagues and facilitate small cohorts of faculty. Over time the community's work has transitioned from a course shell in Blackboard, where people could post resources and samples of work, and engage in discussion via threaded discussions, to the launch of a Community ePortfolio in Spring 2011. A fifteen-member MePort Facilitation team, made up of the early faculty innovators, develops modules to support the faculty learning communities with some structure for faculty learning. These modules are based on the principles of andragogy and are hands-on and practical. In essence, the aim is to provide faculty with the tools they need to be successful in their ePortfolio practice. Because of the rich supports available through the community, there has been a deepening of engagement among faculty with ePortfolios. Two of Mercy's five academic schools adopted schoolwide ePortfolio implementations in fall 2011.

One of the key areas of focus for the learning community is reflection. The community studies what it means to integrate reflection into the teaching and learning process. In addition, reflective prompts are posed to members at the end of every learning community gathering. These questions motivate participants to consider what the highlight of the session was for them, what they are taking away from the session, and what needs remain unmet. Not only do these prompts provide a way for participants to consider how they will use the information and materials in their own ePortfolio work, but they also provide important feedback to the facilitators for future sessions. Developing a learning community where instructors can find resources and support for their ePortfolio implementation is an effective and engaging way to encourage ePortfolio development across the campus. In the case of Mercy College, the learning community concept was a good fit for their institutional context. It also engaged faculty in the reflective practice of documenting evidence of their own transformational, deeper learning experiences which engages faculty in the same ePortfolio work and practices instructors wish for their students.

Engaging Faculty Instructors in ePortfolio Work

As these three examples demonstrate, it is important to situate ePortfolio work within its intended campus context. In some cases, such as Virginia Tech, existing workshops might provide an opening for ePortfolio thinking—a way to engage faculty in thinking about documenting learning in the context of another workshop designed around technology implementation. In other cases, new approaches might need to be developed, such as the Assessment Sketch used at Western Governors, to support faculty in addressing a call for documentation of learning. Learning communities are also a way for faculty to work with peers toward a common goal of designing and sustaining an ePortfolio intervention in a way that is supported and engaging for both faculty and students. The important thing to remember is to develop ways to engage instructors in this kind of redesign that fits with the existing culture of a campus as well as the pedagogical philosophies that are important to them. Knowing who your stakeholders are is central to this process, and looking for ways to partner with others on your campus who have similar or complementary goals is an effective strategy for engaging instructors in documenting learning.

Table 7.1 Implications for Faculty Development Programming to Support ePortfolio Implementation

Implementation Step	Guiding Questions
Learning Outcomes	Are there learning outcomes identified for the campus as a whole or for individual programs (i.e., in strategic planning documents) that ePortfolios can enhance and support? What opportunities and incentives are available on your campus (in terms of consulting or existing workshops) to engage faculty members to think through the ways that their goals for courses or programs map to wider institutional needs and the ways that ePortfolios might support how those outcomes are achieved?
Stakeholders	Who might be interested in ePortfolios on your campus and how might they be partners and sources of support? How can faculty development initiatives be designed such that stakeholders are engaged in both the planning and implementation stages of your ePortfolio project? How can you help faculty instructors foster student buy-in for using ePortfolios? How can faculty design ePortfolio activities that speak to their students' needs? Incorporating an ePortfolio component may require additional technical resources (e.g., IT support and technology training) as well as pedagogical support (e.g., release time and seed grants to redesign a class)—what strategies can be used to generate buy-in to the ePortfolio concept and garner the support required to be successful?
Learning Activities	How can you guide faculty instructors to think through how ePortfolios might enhance their current learning activities? How can you help them consider whether existing assignments or a final project might be a space to implement ePortfolios (in particular, activities that have a reflective component or aim to track progress and development during the course might be good places to start)? What models for redesigning learning activities to introduce ePortfolios currently exist (i.e., are there "early-adopters" on your campus or in the wider ePortfolio community that you can reference as role models)?
Assessment	Given the current methods for assessing student learning (e.g., exams, papers, projects) used on the campus, what additional insights would an ePortfolio approach reveal about a student's learning, particularly their process of learning? Are there approaches already being implemented on your campus that the ePortfolio project might link to? How might assessment strategies used with ePortfolios provide data that are useful to other campus stakeholders?
ePortfolio Tools and Technologies	What features are necessary to allow instructors to effectively manage student ePortfolios (e.g., accessing them, providing feedback, evaluating them)? What support is available and what training is needed for both instructors and students? Where are there opportunities to partner with other campus stakeholders to provide this support?
Evaluation of Impact	What kinds of evidence is desired or needed to evaluate the success of the ePortfolio initiative? How will you support faculty instructors in deciding whether the additional time and investment were worth it? How can you support them in developing an evaluation plan that will help them make the case to a department chair or dean as well as students that this initiative is worth continuing? Some examples might include increased retention, student voices and advocacy, and authentic evidence of the enhancement of skills related to the learning outcomes.

Important Considerations

- Establish a sense of the culture of your campus before your begin. Consult strategic documents, talk to stakeholders who might be interested in documenting learning, and look for points of convergence between their needs and your learning outcomes.
- Look for ways to get faculty to buy-in to the initiative by exploring ways that ePortfolios can support the work that they are already doing in their classrooms.
- Develop programming that fits with both the needs of faculty and the cultural context in which they are working. These might be focused workshops, course design templates, or one-on-one consulting. Remember, you will get people to buy-in to the initiative by making implementation easy and effective for them.

8

Selecting ePortfolio Technologies to Support Learning

The earlier chapters of this book have discussed at length the importance of prioritizing the pedagogy of ePortfolios, which involves clearly defining the learning outcomes to be achieved and establishing a strong foundation for an ePortfolio initiative designed to document student learning. Once these aims are identified, faculty instructors need to consider how the ePortfolio can be implemented to achieve the stated goals.

As with any change in educational practice, the actual challenges come in the implementation stage, particularly when considering which technological tools will best support learners. For example, the academic process of writing a paper changed dramatically with the introduction of new communication and collaboration tools utilizing computers and the Internet. It is almost hard to remember the days when carbon paper needed to be inserted into a manual typewriter in order to have an extra copy of a written paper to share—not to mention the time when manuscripts were produced by scribes. Similarly, when course or learning management systems first entered the higher education market it took many years for both students and faculty instructors to fully understand the implications of the systems' features for curriculum design and course activities and, consequently, change their behaviors and habits in order to reap the benefits of these technological tools.

More recently, it is becoming easier for individuals to quickly adapt to new technologies, largely due to the prevalence of technology in our society and our daily lives. The mobile phones that the majority of students carry with them at all times can serve multiple functions, such as capturing a video of a performance or a photo of an experiment in a scientific lab, and, if web-enabled, they can also be used to upload these artifacts into the student's ePortfolio.

Given the ubiquitous nature of technology today, it is not surprising that ePortfolio tools have been designed not only to support the simple capture of artifacts and reflections but also to allow users to create individual subsets of ePortfolio artifacts, visualize artifact collections, and easily share and archive multimedia content with different audiences. Yet simply being able to do these things does not necessarily result in an effective or efficient ePortfolio implementation.

In this chapter we explore the ways that ePortfolio tools can support the documentation of student learning. First, we describe several issues that are useful to keep in mind when selecting an ePortfolio tool. Second, we consider some of the reasons why ePortfolios are useful in documenting student learning. Finally, we explore some of the technological features that might be desirable, particularly in a pilot project, and how different campuses have chosen tools based on their learning outcomes and how those features helped them meet those outcomes.

The critical takeaway from this chapter is the connection between clearly articulated learning outcomes and the selection of an ePortfolio tool that makes sense for your specific goals and the context of your institution. In short, any tool can be used effectively if the outcomes and pedagogical approach are clearly defined. Successful ePortfolio systems are built upon a folio thinking culture that is not dependent on any particular ePortfolio technology but on how the affordances of the tool relate to the curriculum and address the specific learning outcomes and the needs of the institution and various stakeholder groups.

ISSUES TO CONSIDER FOR ePORTFOLIO TOOL SELECTION

The emphasis on establishing a culture of folio thinking is a critical first step in establishing an ePortfolio initiative. The selection of an ePortfolio technology should be informed by a clear understanding of stakeholders and their needs and contextualized within the process of implementing ePortfolios. Factors that are critical in the planning stages related to the selection of ePortfolio technology include:

Context: What is the department, program, or institutional culture around technology (e.g., course or learning management systems, social media in the classroom)? Will the ePortfolio technology be implemented institution-wide or in individual courses? Will the tool be something that can be easily piloted with one faculty instructor in one course or will it be something that needs to work with the current course or learning management system?

Resources required: Connecting back to the institutional culture, what resources are available for enterprise-wide solutions, Information Technology (IT) support, and so on? Who's funding this ePortfolio initiative? What kinds of tools are being evaluated—commercial vendors, open source, Web 2.0, or Internet based? In addition to technical support, as instructors consider how to redesign their courses and activities to incorporate an ePortfolio component, they may also need release time and pedagogical guidance from organizations such as campus centers for teaching and learning, or incentives through grant programs, travel, funds, and the like.

Additional factors may include how well the tool meets the students' and faculty's skill levels and competence, and how it fits with the culture of the campus. Faculty instructors will also want to be clear on the learning outcomes they are seeking, the range of artifacts demonstrating the work they want their students to create and accompany with meaningful reflections, and the strategies they will use to assess students at both formative and summative stages. How the ePortfolio effort is presented to students will also convey how the faculty and the institution view and value students' efforts in this undertaking. Similarly, for faculty, introducing the concept of an ePortfolio and framing it as a tool aimed to specifically address their needs and concerns also comes with the commensurate amount of support and preparation time to adapt and adopt this new model that will be critical to a successful launch.

Key Reasons for Using ePortfolio Tools

As discussed throughout this book, there is wide acknowledgment of the need for better evidence of actual student learning beyond grades and credit hours. An informal review of ePortfolio systems currently being used by educational communities in higher education was conducted on behalf of the EPAC community of practice in spring 2011 by Professor J. Elizabeth Clark of LaGuardia

Community College (EPAC, 2011). Although not a comprehensive study, the preliminary findings suggest that institutions are looking to ePortfolios to support the documentation of learning in general education and the disciplines and viewing ePortfolios as an alternative to standardized tests that may result in more authentic evidence to support integrative and interdisciplinary learning.

Increasingly, pressure from accreditation bodies, policymakers, and institutional stakeholders such as parents and donors has prompted institutions to look to ePortfolios in order to gain a deeper understanding of what students are getting out of their educational experiences. There is also a growing need to assess the learning of transfer students, adult learners returning to school, and nontraditional students; ePortfolios are one method being promoted for prior learning assessment by groups such as the Center for Adult and Experiential Learning (CAEL).

In some cases, the requirements for better evidence are represented by a top-down mandate from the administration. However, the concept of an ePortfolio that is created and managed by students over the course of their educational career implies benefits to the students themselves as they capture their work, not in a three-ring binder, but in an environment that facilitates digital curation of their collection of artifacts, reflection, and presentation of selected work to external audiences. Students, faculty, administrators, employers, and parents note that this type of documentation can provide opportunities for career and professional development, not only for students but also for faculty instructors, graduate students, and post-doctoral researchers. Teaching portfolios for graduate students and young faculty are not uncommon; ePortfolios are also used in professional areas such as accounting and financial management, nursing, midwifery, and other the health fields.

Course/Learning Management Needs   Independent ePortfolio tools including commercial, open source, and web-based options such as blogs, wikis, and Google Sites can also be used to address course or learning management needs. However, though these tools can work quite well for a pilot or an individual class, scalability and sustainability over time can be challenging without the additional administrative features that allow faculty to easily find and track updates to student ePortfolios during the academic term.

Institutional or Programmatic Assessment Accreditation or program cre-dentialing are also oft-cited reasons for wanting to use ePortfolios. However, though many tools provide opportunities to collect evidence of student work, additional functionalities and services are often needed to manage data for evalu-ation activities, such as the process of sampling artifacts representative of learning outcomes for evaluation by multiple external reviewers using rubrics.

Although in many ways related, these various reasons for using ePortfolios can result in a list of desirable features believed to be needed for a successful implementation. Indeed, many campuses have multiple requirements and out-comes that they want ePortfolios to address. However, no tool will meet every need perfectly, making it important to explore and prioritize the key features of an ePortfolio tool in relation to the outcomes that you want to address.

Key Features of ePortfolio Tools and Current Practices

Though not exhaustive, the following criteria highlight some of the key features that institutions weigh and prioritize when exploring possible ePortfolio tools for piloting and adoption.

Usability Usability of the ePortfolio and its interface is one critical considera-tion, especially when introducing the tool to students, faculty, staff, and anyone else who might possibly look at the ePortfolio, such as prospective employers, graduate school admission committees, family, and friends. From the perspective of the ePortfolio owner and creator, the interface must be user friendly, easy to use, navigate, and customize, and be aesthetically pleasing. A professional look and feel is especially important for students who may already have accounts with commercial web sites. In order to encourage student ownership of an ePortfolio that goes beyond simply uploading documents to fulfill a requirement or class assignment, institutions must be prepared for ePortfolios to be compared to such web sites as Facebook and LinkedIn. Technologically savvy students increasingly understand the importance of having a professional online presence and, unlike commercial web sites or a web site built using Google Sites with a personalized URL, the institutional brand and reputation of the education in which students have invested both time and money has value, both to the student and the insti-tution. To this end, a plan for continuing access to the ePortfolio after graduation is essential, and this is perhaps where engaging in conversations with the campus alumni association would be fruitful, as they have an interest and a stake in continuing to sustain and support a strong relationship between alumni and the institution.

San Francisco State University (SFSU) has worked to address these issues in their ePortfolio implementations. Since 2005, the Master of Public Health program in Community Health Education at SFSU has used eFolio (http://www.efolioworld .com/), a hosted solution, to facilitate student documentation of evidence in the form of signature assignments, multimedia presentations, and so on from academic courses, practicum, and culminating experience projects. In addition to supporting both self-assessment and external evaluation by advisors, peers, faculty committee members, and members of the community, students were also encouraged to "utilize ePortfolios to showcase their skills in public health practice for further academic and professional development and international outreach as public health professionals" in order to support future employment opportunities (http://healthed.sfsu.edu/mph.aspx#ePort). Figure 8.1 prominently features the student's achievements and coursework as well as the program and institutional brand. The eFolio tool provided students with a way to showcase their learning in a highly usable way.

The use of Adobe Acrobat Professional to create ePortfolios in a PDF format that is easily accessible with the free Acrobat Reader, as shown in Figure 8.2, represents another technology option that provides students with a usable solution to create ePortfolios. At Clemson University, a Landscape and Architecture class conducted a three-week pilot project to illustrate how the competency requirements of the university could be showcased in this platform for prospective employers. The ability of Adobe Acrobat Professional to package multiple PDFs allowed the students to quickly build upon work completed earlier in the course and from previous classes to create unique and personalized PDF ePortfolios that could be easily shared with employers.

Student Control   Because one of the signature aspects of ePortfolios is the ability of the learner to document what it is that they know, understand, or are able to do, and the development of those skills and abilities, the ePortfolio tool should emphasize a learner-centered view of education (as opposed to a course, faculty, or

Figure 8.1   Master of Public Health ePortfolio

Source: San Francisco State University, http://savitamalik.efolioworld.com/Introduction

institution focus). It is important for students to be able to truly make their ePortfolio their own through the selection of what pieces of work to include, deciding who to share their ePortfolio with (or creating multiple ePortfolios or different views of their ePortfolio depending on the audience), and using the tool as a creative outlet to include activities and achievements enabled by the educational environment and opportunities but which are not easily labeled or categorized on a résumé or transcript. Many tools provide the opportunity to either use templates to guide learners as students create their ePortfolios or allow them to create their own structure. Blogging and web site creation tools are popular with students because they can create and customize their ePortfolios in order to document their learning. For instance, the music education program at the Pennsylvania State University incorporates the design and development of ePortfolios as part of the educational development of its students throughout their program (see Figure 8.3). Though students are required to incorporate specific types of evidence into their ePortfolios at particular milestones in their program, the tools provide them with the flexibility of creating ePortfolios that reflect their personalities, skills, and abilities.

Integration with the Course/Learning Management System Although many tools can provide learners with the opportunity to have control over the content of their ePortfolios, it is often the case that ePortfolio artifacts are created in the context of classroom-based learning. Therefore, an increasingly important feature of ePortfolio tools is their ability to integrate with the campus course/learning management system. Given the growing number of functionalities, many ePortfolio tools are available as an additional module or feature set offered as part of commercial

Figure 8.2   PDF ePortfolio

Source: Clemson University

course or learning management system (CMS/LMS) or virtual learning environment (VLE). One advantage of an integrated ePortfolio service within the CMS/LMS that is already in place is that it eases the adoption process for students, faculty, and instructors. Some examples include Desire2Learn and Blackboard's ePortfolio modules and the use of the open source Moodle CMS/LMS with the Mahara ePortfolio, which are typically locally installed and supported by information technology (IT) staff.

Support Resources   Whether the ePortfolio tool that is chosen is an enterprise or campuswide ePortfolio installation, purchased or open source, or a cloud-based solution such as Yola, Weebly, or WordPress, it is important to ensure that the appropriate support resources are made available to those who are implementing them as well as those who are using them. In hosted versus cloud-based ePortfolio platforms as well as open source versus proprietary solutions, there are costs for the institution and for the students, especially with respect to how various stakeholders are trained in using ePortfolios and the resources that are available to

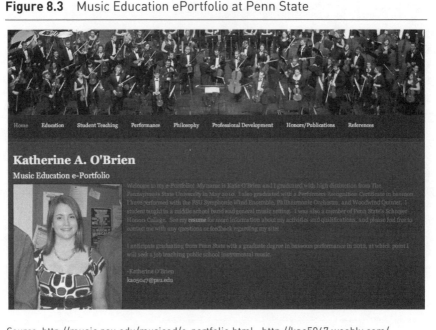

them on campus and from the vendor or user community. Careful consideration of the various types of support resources that are required to meet the intended outcomes of the ePortfolio implementation and ensuring that those resources are in place for users is an important step to ensure success. For instance, Salt Lake Community College offers one-credit courses on essential computer skills and an "ePortfolios for Success" course that help students to begin the process of creating an ePortfolio. LaGuardia Community College provides online instructional guides and video tutorials for faculty and students as well as open lab hours at their dedicated ePortfolio Studio equipped with hardware and software, and supported by instructional design assistants, student technology mentors, and ePortfolio consultants. At San Francisco State University the Teaching and Learning Group offers comprehensive and tailored pedagogical and technical support for faculty and students as they develop the technical and cognitive skills associated with creating and evaluating media-rich ePortfolios. There, students are trained in

90-minute sessions in "gateway" courses identified by each department. Over the years, it has been noted that the most successful departments to deploy ePortfolios have been those that have required the completion of a "gateway" course tied to ePortfolio use. Successful projects are able to follow a sequential structure that allows Academic Technology to issue ePortfolio accounts to all students through the "gateway" courses, promote full-faculty buy-in by expecting the timely uploading of "signature" assignments each term, and require finishing the portfolios in a capstone identified course.

Interoperability Another instructional and technical consideration is how ePortfolios can be effectively transferred from one institution to another. Prior efforts have included IMS Global Learning Consortium's ePortfolio specifications developed in 2005. More recently, given the growing mobility among today's students in part due to increased access to higher education through online learning, in spring 2010, the Postsecondary Electronic Standards Council (PESC) launched an Academic ePortfolio Workgroup to specifically investigate the use of academic ePortfolios as "e-transcripts" and to establish "interoperability standards and data sharing capabilities that would allow today's typically mobile learners . . . to easily take their Academic e-Portfolio with them wherever they happen to enroll and learn." (See PESC web site: http://www.pesc.org/interior.php?page_id=209.) This is important, for instance, when ePortfolios are used to grant transfer credits when learners move from one educational institution to another. In addition, given that sometimes an ePortfolio tool chosen at one moment in time may not meet future needs, it is important to be able to transfer student artifacts between institutional systems. Interoperability is also important for career development. Upon graduation, learners may want to take their institutional ePortfolio to their workplace, which may have its own ePortfolio tool. For instance, some accounting and financial management students at the University of Waterloo who developed ePortfolios to document "soft skills" as part of their academic program found that co-op employers had their own ePortfolio-type systems for documenting workplace learning. This revelation has led the School of Accounting and Finance to work with the Centre for Co-operative Education to dialogue with employers about the types of tools being used to document learning in the profession and the ways that evidence can be transferred between tools. Considering the issue of interoperability up front, particularly in terms of the ways that ePortfolios might be practically used by learners and institutions, can inform the planning of effective implementations and the selection of appropriate tools.

Security, Plagiarism, and Storage   Security, plagiarism, and storage are three areas that many institutions are concerned about. It is crucial to maintain privacy and the integrity of intellectual property and academic authenticity, particularly as students are frequently asked to upload and share their work through online means and as institutions use ePortfolio technology to document, record, and evaluate their learning. Western Governors University (WGU), a private, nonprofit, fully online university founded by the governors of nineteen western states, provides some insight into these issues. Designed as a competency-based institution, WGU has used the ePortfolio tools available from TaskStream, LLC, for the better part of a decade and has found ePortfolios to be one of the most authentic, robust, and useful methods available. In addition to security, it is also necessary to defend against plagiarism. WGU takes advantage of TaskStream's integration of Turnitin.com, which provides automatic screening of student ePortfolio submissions for potential originality problems. Caveon Web-Patrol is another part of the security and privacy protocols employed as part of the protection of ePortfolios.

In addition to security systems and other technological solutions, WGU's institutional culture and views toward these issues are communicated to faculty through information and training provided on the Family Educational and Privacy Act of 1974 (FERPA) and dealing with threats to academic authenticity. The digital nature of ePortfolios makes them more susceptible to various forms of academic dishonesty. Though faculty do not need to be deterred by this fact, they should be aware in order to protect against it. Institutions would be wise to seek out guidance on strategies that can help prevent the likelihood of academic dishonesty. Essay mills, tutoring sites, and ghostwriters are some of the threats that are currently alive and well. The credibility of the degrees that students attain from colleges and universities is directly related to the integrity of the examinations and other demonstrations of learning. Therefore, preserving that integrity is central to the success and longevity of each institution. It is important to consider the issues of security and plagiarism in terms of the functionality provided by ePortfolio tools to support academic and institutional integrity. This is also an important instructional design issue that faculty instructors must consider when developing ePortfolio activities for students to complete in order to document their learning (see Chapter Four).

Given the variety of ePortfolio artifacts that can be created and used to document learning, it is important to consider what the needs will be for reliable archival and storage. Because ePortfolios are truly electronic, they exist in cyberspace, which can experience problems and calamities just like actual physical spaces. Therefore, there is a significant need to protect ePortfolios from virtual disasters, just as it is necessary to protect student records from natural disasters. At WGU, for instance, several means are employed to protect all data and student learning documentation, including ePortfolios, from technical mishaps. To this end, WGU employs multiple redundancies and other data preservation methods to ensure that no data or student artifacts are lost or destroyed. It is important for any institution considering the use of ePortfolios to take precautions to protect data and student artifacts.

Assessment   The need to protect data and student artifacts is particularly critical when ePortfolios are being used as an assessment tool. In the last decade, ePortfolio features and associated services related to student assessment have largely become a required component of any ePortfolio platform. This may include the integration of rubrics, aggregation and disaggregation of data, and easy generation of reports at the individual student, class, department, program, and institutional levels. At the same time, the definition of what constitutes evidence of student learning has been expanded to include not just numbers and grades but multimedia artifacts and reflections that are not only summative in nature but also provide formative feedback to students, faculty, and institutions. Another result of taking a learner-centered approach is a broader, longer-term perspective that reaches beyond the final product to provide insight into the process of learning as facilitated by folio thinking. Though the ePortfolio technology can facilitate this, how this new wealth of data and information is processed and used to inform decisions in the classroom, student policies, curriculum requirements, and so on is still being figured out.

The use of ePortfolios to address some of the student assessment needs described above has been explored at California State University, Fullerton (CSUF), the third largest university in California and, for the past decade, the number-one destination for transfer students from California's community colleges. CSUF has a strong commitment to underrepresented students and is the only four-year, comprehensive Hispanic-Serving Institution (HSI) in Orange County and is also an Asian American and Pacific Islander–Serving Institution (AAPI).

The goals of this collaborative endeavor of faculty, students, and administrators around ePortfolios are to:

1. Demonstrate the alignment of multiple levels of student learning outcomes, such that there is a link from course assignment through to university student learning outcomes;

2. Utilize this curriculum map for data collection and assessment of student artifacts;

3. Balance diversity and standardization in such a way that assessment program research design reflects the discipline in which the student and faculty are engaged while benefiting from interdisciplinary perspectives and expertise;

4. Incorporate community partners into the assessment process; and

5. Disseminate the findings.

A major emphasis of the university is to use and highlight ePortfolios as the means to capture evidence of learning (documentation of academic achievement) and to determine how such evidence leads to ongoing change and improvement. Through the Epsilen Learning Matrix (ELM) student work is archived and accessed by faculty assessment teams. A flexible structure means that faculty can design the web-based learning matrix to meet the needs of a program- or course-level assessment project. Published or faculty-developed rubrics are linked to each student-learning outcome, and the rubric can be viewed by students and by faculty reviewers. Students have the ability to upload faculty-directed artifacts in multiple media formats such as written documents, videos, podcasts or other audio recordings, or images. The ability to include external stakeholders in assessment makes ePortfolios a strong tool for integrating community engagement into the curriculum. Additionally, many departments and programs have additional requirements for assessment related to accreditation that include a review by external evaluators. It is anticipated that the ability to engage reviewers outside of the academic environment will be an effective method for supporting students in accomplishing their educational and professional goals. Many participating departments include faculty who wish to pilot the use of the learning matrix for course-level assessment that is integrated with faculty-student collaborative research or outreach activities coordinated with community partners through internships or service learning.

Faculty teams are also examining using this system for formative assessment—how students improve over their time at CSUF—and for summative assessment—how students perform at the completion of their degree programs. In addition to student-learning artifacts, assessment strategies include the collection of additional information to be used for program improvement to support a diverse student body. These data are linked to the learning matrix and structured so that departments and the university can address value-added questions, such as comparing differences in the achievement of student learning outcomes by students from varied backgrounds. It is expected that the time to graduation will decrease through more effective advisement that incorporates the data from formative assessment, such as how courses taken by a student to date meet department and university student learning outcomes. By integrating assessment with the university's LMS, these data will be available to advisors and students in real time as a continually updated monitor of learning outcome achievement. As students complete their degree, the prediction is that summative assessment and student ePortfolios will enhance job and professional advancement by serving as e-résumés and supplements to social networking.

The Epsilen ePortfolio Pilot project in Figure 8.4 is innovative in that it combines numerous aspects of assessment with curriculum development, advisement, and research, and encourages student-ownership through e-résumés and professional networking. Furthermore, it has the capacity to allow faculty to integrate their research and teaching with student assessment, emphasizing assessment as a primary activity of teacher-scholars.

Although some of the key features of ePortfolio tools have been highlighted here in relation to many of the reasons for using ePortfolios, it is important to remember that the tool is really incidental to the pedagogical approach and learning outcomes that it is meant to support. Technology is rapidly changing and it is unlikely that any one tool will perfectly match all the needs of a given institution. Other emerging technical features that are garnering more attention

Figure 8.4   Epsilen ePortfolio

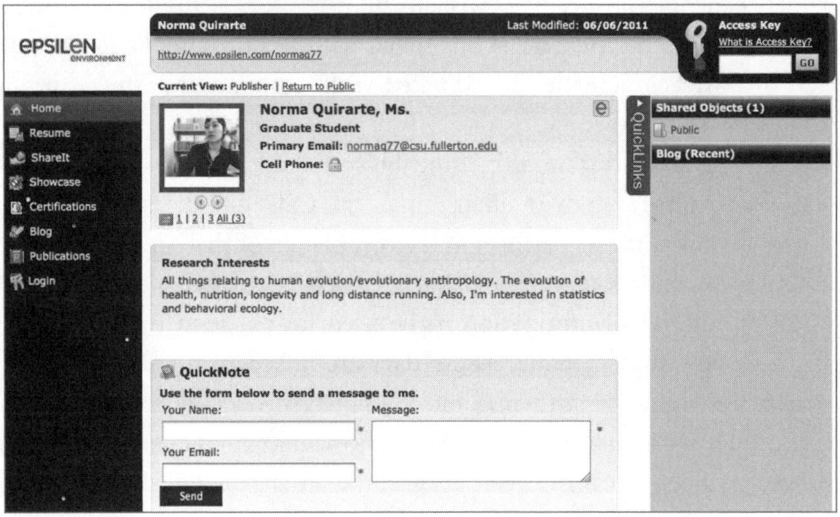

Source: Norma Quirarte, CSU Fullerton, http://www.epsilen.com/normaq77

are the social networking features either embedded within the ePortfolio through commenting capabilities or links to Facebook or Twitter; the ability to tag artifacts or posts in order to easily access them in the future (as opposed to using simple search functions); visualization of artifact collections through interactive knowledge or networking maps or word clouds; and greater support for multimedia artifacts.

What is important to remember is the need to develop a clear framework for choosing an ePortfolio tool for your context that will allow you to most efficiently meet your stated outcomes. As the examples presented here highlight, any tool can be used effectively if the outcomes or pedagogical approach are clearly defined in the context of the institutional culture and its stakeholders and their needs. Successful ePortfolio systems built upon a folio thinking culture are not dependent on the particular ePortfolio tool that is selected but on how the affordances of the tool relate to the curriculum and address the critical needs of the institution and various stakeholder groups.

Table 8.1 Implications for the Selection of Tools to Support an ePortfolio Implementation

Implementation Step	Guiding Questions
Learning Outcomes	Given the desired goals and learning outcomes for this ePortfolio initiative, what is the vision for how the ePortfolio and its specific features can help the project leaders and participants achieve these learning outcomes?
Stakeholders	Who will be using the ePortfolio tool—with respect to those creating the ePortfolios and those who will wish to view the artifacts that are collected? The needs and characteristics of your stakeholders—how technologically savvy they are, whether they have access to the Internet, whether they are on or off campus, and so on—have implications for not only the tool but also the resources to train and support these users. How does the value of the ePortfolio get communicated to students? Are all possible stakeholders (including students, faculty, IT staff, community members, campus registrars, and so on) represented on the committee to select ePortfolio tool(s)?
Learning Activities	How will the ePortfolio actually be incorporated into class assignments and other activities? How does the ePortfolio tool capture and organize various kinds of artifacts collected over time? Are there administrative features that can help instructors easily access student ePortfolios, create reports, identify missing assignments, and so on?
Assessment	Will managing student assessment data and evidence be a desired feature of the ePortfolio tool? What is the current process of assessment and how can an ePortfolio facilitate that process, e.g., by using rubrics to evaluate samples of student work collected from multiple courses and programs? Rather than students simply turning in assignments to faculty, can the ePortfolio help students build a collection of assignments and artifacts which both they and the faculty can access and review?
ePortfolio Tools and Technologies	Though the focus of this table is primarily on the selection of an ePortfolio tool, the implications of technology relate specifically to evidence—what is the nature and range of evidence that will be captured, reviewed, accessed by multiple people, and archived? Key to this effort is understanding the "value added" of an *electronic* portfolio tool vs. students simply completing assignments on paper or turning in files via e-mail or the CMS/LMS.
Evaluation of Impact	The adoption of an ePortfolio technology can be a significant investment although many free and low-cost Web 2.0 tools are available for individual course pilots, and so forth. Giving thought to the markers of success for your ePortfolio initiative as a whole during your early planning stages is a fruitful exercise. For example, will you measure success by the rate of adoption, number of user accounts, interest from key faculty members, and so on?

Important Considerations

- Start with clearly defined learning outcomes and then thoroughly explore and engage with various ePortfolio vendors; see demos, evaluate their features, and experiment with different tools to find out whether they will allow students to document their learning in a way that meets your outcomes and goals.
- Seek out institutions or programs that are similar to yours and find out what is working for them and how they are meeting their learning goals with particular tools.
- Talk to stakeholders about their needs and have them test different tools and provide feedback. For example, how a student interacts with a tool is often very different from how the faculty instructor might do so—take into consideration the tool's interfaces for various ePortfolio users and purposes.
- Find out what resources are available on campus to support the tool that is chosen.
- One size does *not* fit all—it may be very likely that a suite of ePortfolio tools is a better fit for the needs of specific disciplines and programs. Find the right balance between stakeholder needs and institutional resources.

Evaluating the Impact of ePortfolios

The ePortfolio implementation framework introduced at the beginning of this book outlines the necessary steps to consider in order to plan a successful ePortfolio initiative, starting with establishing a clear definition of the learning goals and outcomes for the project and moving on to various tasks related to the design of relevant learning activities, the selection of ePortfolio technology, and so on. Although the evaluation of the impact of ePortfolios is listed as the last step in this iterative process, in reality, planning for evaluation should run parallel with the tasks of the implementation framework.

The evaluation phase is based on a more holistic view of the ePortfolio effort. It should apply the same folio thinking process to the entire project, essentially creating a project ePortfolio aimed at gathering artifacts to document that the initiative successfully achieved its stated goals and desired outcomes. The critical component of the evaluation of impact is the issue of evidence. As posed in the implementation framework: What kinds of evidence are needed for the various stakeholders to validate the investment of time and resources to implement ePortfolios? How might the documentation of learning collected in ePortfolios be used by other stakeholders on your campus (i.e., in accreditation efforts)? How will you *evaluate* whether or not your ePortfolio initiative was a success?

As noted in the Introduction, a useful activity proposed by Richard L. Venezky (2001) known as the history of the future exercise encourages project leaders to clearly articulate the project goals so that a relevant evaluation plan can be designed to specifically address the desired outcomes.

History of the Future Exercise

Imagine that your ePortfolio project is completed and that it has succeeded in all of its goals. You are to appear tomorrow at a press conference to explain what you have accomplished. Write a press release for distributing at this meeting, explaining in a few paragraphs what it is that you have accomplished, who is benefiting from ePortfolios, why they are important tools for documenting learning (what problem does their use solve and why did it need to be solved in the first place?), and what it was that you did that led to or caused this success.

Source: Adapted from Venezky, 2001, p.18.

As we suggested in the Introduction, by completing this exercise at the beginning of a project and revisiting it periodically, the desired outcomes and deliverables can serve as a destination and a touchstone to inform the design of the initiative and to ensure that the project is on the right path. It can be particularly helpful to project leaders as talking points to reference when explaining what the desired outcomes are, why they are important, and how they can be achieved. The ability to plan, monitor, and control the project by articulating the outcomes is an essential facet of any ePortfolio project.

Using a backward design approach, this statement of expected outcomes for the ePortfolio project informs the plan and the strategies for achieving these project or programmatic goals. Instead of looking at the impact of ePortfolios on an individual student, the focus is on the project or program level and may encompass such issues as how the ePortfolio changes faculty and student perspectives on teaching and learning, funding priorities for pedagogical innovations and curriculum redesign, and the availability of resources and support for experimentation with new technologies in the classroom. Clear articulation of outcomes at every stage of the project is necessary in order to ensure that the ePortfolio initiative has a positive impact for all stakeholders at all levels. Although we have discussed the possibility of building a project ePortfolio, this may actually be an "evidence of impact" ePortfolio that scaffolds reflection on the project and guides the project leaders through a process of folio thinking that parallels what the students and faculty experience.

DATA COLLECTION METHODS

Table 9.1 reiterates our emphasis on documenting learning to demonstrate and evaluate the effects of an ePortfolio initiative (Chen and Penny Light, 2010) by illustrating the range of data that already exists that can be unobtrusively gathered without too much additional effort. The key is in planning ahead and recognizing who might own these data and how to go about accessing this information. Given who your project stakeholders are, it may be important to consider what kinds of data they would find persuasive and compelling, such as student voices expressed in the ePortfolio, national statistics on ePortfolio adoption, or examples of what peer and aspirant institutions are doing with ePortfolios.

Although the Inter/National Coalition for Electronic Portfolio Research has been bringing together cohorts of institutions since 2003, there is increasing national recognition of ePortfolio work and governmental support for such initiatives. In 2007, LaGuardia Community College with support from the Fund for the Improvement of Postsecondary Education (FIPSE) launched

Table 9.1 Methods for Collecting Evidence of Impact

Environmental Methods	• Usage logs of how often the ePortfolio tool was accessed, types of activities, and amount of time spent in the environment • Review of budgets, allocations of funds • Total number of ePortfolio accounts created • Attendance at ePortfolio training sessions and other ePortfolio community events (e.g., speakers, faculty coffees or get-togethers, both face-to-face and online) • Conference presentations, posters, and other publications • Press articles and blog postings about the pilot
Indirect Methods	• Surveys of faculty and students on various teaching and learning-related outcomes such as engagement, intention to continue using the ePortfolio, perceptions of value and usefulness of the ePortfolio • Post-training evaluations of training sessions • Measures of satisfaction, continuing interest • Interviews with various stakeholders • Identification of ePortfolio advocates by students, faculty, and staff
Direct Methods	• Case studies created from interviews with faculty on how they introduced ePortfolios to their students, what did and didn't work • Examples of assignments created, reflective prompts • Faculty assessment results • Anecdotal stories of how ePortfolios have been used

the Making Connections National Resource Center with thirty New York City higher education institutions to help them develop ePortfolio pilots for enhanced engagement, learning, and assessment. This project was followed by the five-year Making Transfer Connections project funded through a Title V grant partnering two senior colleges and three community colleges in the use of ePortfolios to facilitate transfer and ensure student progress toward the bachelor's degree. In 2011, FIPSE again awarded LaGuardia Community College a grant to establish the *Connect to Learning: ePortfolio, Engagement and Student Success* project which has partnered with the Association for Authentic Experiential and Evidence-Based Learning (AAEEBL) to build a national network among twenty-two campuses—community colleges, private colleges, and research universities—to collectively contribute to the design of an empirically informed model for ePortfolio development. Another FIPSE-supported project begun in 2011 is the *Integrative Knowledge Collaborative* led by Dr. Melissa Peet of the University of Michigan and involving partnerships with several higher education institutions and technology organizations. This project employs the Integrative Knowledge Portfolio Process and Generative Knowledge Interviewing method (Peet et al., 2011) to identify and showcase best practices for educating lifelong learners and leaders.

Each of these projects shares a common goal of establishing a national network of institutions and contributing to the research and knowledge of ePortfolios as a discipline. Another example of the scholarly impact of ePortfolios on higher education is the *International Journal of ePortfolio*, a publication of the Center for Instructional Development and Educational Research at Virginia Tech, which released its first issue in fall 2011. The venues for dissemination of ePortfolio findings continue to expand through numerous communication sites and national and international networks including the American Association of Colleges and Universities (AAC&U), AAEEBL, EPAC, Australia's ePortfolio Community of Practice, and the European Institute for eLearning (EIfeL) to name but a few. As a result, the impact of any individual institution's work can be amplified, and opportunities for the exploration of these cross-cutting questions and issues of interest with like-minded colleagues from around the world are truly unlimited.

Table 9.2   Implications for Evaluating the Impact of Your ePortfolio Initiative

Implementation Step	Guiding Questions
Learning Outcomes	Based on the "history of the future" exercise, what are the desired goals and outcomes for this ePortfolio initiative? What do you hope this project will achieve not only for the individual students and faculty who are directly involved but for the other stakeholders who have invested in this initiative?
Stakeholders	Which parties do you expect this ePortfolio initiative to influence and benefit, aside from those stakeholders who are directly involved (e.g., faculty and students)? Who else on campus has a "stake" in whether this project succeeds or fails?
Learning Activities	Given the time line for your ePortfolio project (whether it's a pilot for one course or part of a first-year experience), how will you document the progress of the ePortfolio project? One idea might be to create a project ePortfolio to capture findings and reflections.
Assessment	How will you assess whether this ePortfolio project has met the expectations and goals of the various stakeholders? What kinds of artifacts would be useful to capture either within or outside of the ePortfolio and analyze in order to determine which aspects of this project have been successful?
ePortfolio Tools and Technologies	How can the ePortfolio itself be used to guide and scaffold a process of reflection, documentation, and integration by the ePortfolio project leaders for the purpose of showcasing the achievements and impact of the initiative?
Evaluation of Impact	How will you disseminate and promote the emerging findings from this ePortfolio project? The project ePortfolio could be one source but also consider holding workshops and webinars for interested faculty and colleagues both on and off campus, presenting at conferences, publicizing the work in the campus newspaper, and so forth.

Important Considerations

- Be sure to begin thinking about how you will evaluate the impact of your ePortfolio initiative at the *beginning* of the project. Revisit your evaluation plan frequently throughout the project implementation to ensure that you are collecting the data you will need to meet your project goals and stakeholder expectations and needs.
- Keep track of and reflect on the process early and often — refine your evaluation plans as your ePortfolio project unfolds.
- Explore opportunities to collaborate and disseminate your experiences through national and international ePortfolio-related networks, communication channels, and communities of practice.

Conclusion

The Association for American Colleges and Universities (AAC&U) has noted the promise of ePortfolios as a significant and meaningful approach to respond to the increasing pressures of educational accountability. In this book, we have explored the various ways ePortfolios can be employed to document learning. They can help students make connections among the learning that happens in different contexts in order to develop their intellectual and social identities. The development of these identities is critical for today's learners who will live and work in an increasingly globalized and technological world. As such, we believe that we have a moral imperative as educators to ensure that today's students are equipped with the skills to integrate their knowledge and experiences in meaningful ways.

It is important to design significant learning experiences that engage learners in intentional learning—we want them to take ownership for their learning so that they can be conscientious citizens and lifelong learners upon graduation. However, the onus of responsibility for educating these global citizens does not rest solely on educators. The transformation of higher education due to economic, societal, and political pressures will be an incentive to some students to consider a "do-it-yourself" education that includes a combination of formal study, open education, and self-learning (Kamenetz, 2010). This idea is not a new one and reinforces the findings from one of the earliest ePortfolio leaders, Alverno College, whose longitudinal research on student learning and learning outcomes across disciplines demonstrated that "learning that lasts is self-aware and reflective, self-assessed, and self-regarding" (Mentkowski and Associates, 2000, 232–235; Rickards and Guilbault, 2009). Well-designed ePortfolio initiatives represent one approach for supporting the documentation of multiple forms of learning, wherever they may occur, for self-knowledge, integration, and assessment at individual, programmatic, and institutional levels.

With the aim of setting instructors up for success as they design experiences and opportunities for ePortfolio learning, this book outlines a framework for implementing ePortfolios that is iterative in nature and establishes, at the heart of the process, clearly articulated learning outcomes. These outcomes map to the culture and context of an institution and to the pedagogical philosophy of individual instructors while also considering the needs of other stakeholders who might have an interest in supporting and benefiting from an ePortfolio initiative. Arum and Roksa (2011) emphasize the need for colleges and universities to "routinely collect diverse sources of evaluation and assessment data to improve instruction and student learning on an ongoing basis." The evidence that is collected using ePortfolios certainly has the potential to supplement standard survey data from instruments such as the Collegiate Learning Assessment (CLA) and the National Survey of Student Engagement (NSSE) and to promote triangulation and integration among various quantitative and qualitative datasets. The Lumina Foundation for Education's Degree Qualifications Profile (2011), which proposes a template describing the broad skills that students should achieve at each degree level, also has exciting implications for the use of ePortfolios in higher education, particularly for assessment purposes.

The ePortfolio Implementation Framework has served as the touchstone throughout this book and was adapted to the particular issues and needs of each stakeholder group

On the http://www.documentinglearning.com/ web site you can find additional resources and expanded examples of ePortfolios mentioned in this book. Some of these programs are:

- MyPortfolio: A national portfolio service for New Zealand schools
- California State University, Fullerton Epsilen Pilot Project
- San Francisco State University
- Making Learning Visible: Finding Every Learner's Potential: 21st Century Learning with Differentiated Assessment and ePortfolios at Boston University
- ePortfolios in Everyday Education: Western Governors University
- Clemson University using Acrobat Pro and GoogleSites

being addressed. By revisiting this framework in each of the relevant chapters, we hope to have modeled a process by which you can now apply this framework and develop your own guiding questions for other stakeholders who are not addressed in this book. To this end, a web site accompanying this book (http://documentinglearning.com) will provide a space for readers to contribute to a collection of adaptations of this framework including any guiding questions that are useful for additional stakeholders so that they can be shared more broadly with the members of our international ePortfolio community of practice.

We encourage you to carefully think through each of the issues in the framework and to consider how the guiding questions can be answered in your context. The steps in this framework are iterative—project leaders will need to contemplate and revisit the goals of the implementation to ensure that the

Table C.1   ePortfolio Implementation Framework

Implementation Step	Guiding Questions
Defining learning outcomes	What are the **learning outcomes** for your ePortfolio initiative? What types of learning do you want to capture and document?
Identifying and understanding learners and stakeholders	Who are your **stakeholders**, especially your learners (the people who will be creating and using the ePortfolio)? How can they benefit from ePortfolios (i.e., what are their needs)? What can they contribute to and how can they support an ePortfolio effort?
Designing learning activities	Given your outcomes, what **activities** can you design to best guide the ways that learners use the ePortfolio to document their learning? How will their learning be captured and documented in the ePortfolio? How can the artifacts and evidence that are captured be organized, connected, and shared in meaningful and integrated ways?
Informing assessment of student learning	How do the ePortfolios and their artifacts inform **assessment** of student learning? In other words, what evidence is needed for learners to document their achievements and competencies? How can rubrics be used to support ePortfolio assessment?
Using ePortfolio tools and technologies	Which **ePortfolio tools and technologies** will allow you to collect the types of evidence that will allow learners to document and demonstrate their learning? What additional resources are needed (e.g., IT support) in order for your ePortfolio initiative to succeed?
Evaluating the impact of your ePortfolio initiative	What kinds of evidence would validate the investment of time and resources in ePortfolios to all stakeholders? In other words, how might the documentation of learning collected in ePortfolios be used by other stakeholders on your campus (i.e., in accreditation efforts)? How will you **evaluate** whether or not your ePortfolio initiative was a success?

learning outcomes that the ePortfolio initiative is meant to achieve are clear to all of the stakeholders involved. Obviously, the most important stakeholders are the learners themselves—if they are unclear about why they are creating ePortfolios, then the implementation is sure to miss its mark. As noted throughout this book, the process of engaging the relevant stakeholders on a campus, while acknowledging and working within the cultural context of the department, program, and course, is crucial to the success of an ePortfolio initiative. Of course, as noted throughout the book and especially in Chapter Nine, we cannot advocate strongly enough that the pedagogy *must* lead the technology, and the project's desired learning outcomes should serve as the guide and the foundation for any ePortfolio implementation. As you move forward with your ePortfolio initiatives we encourage you to consider early and often how you will evaluate the success of the ePortfolio project, and what changes need to be made in order to ensure that the goals identified at the beginning of the project are being met.

This process, we believe, is relatively straightforward but we also know that no innovation project is ever really that simple. It is important to keep in mind that bumps in the road will occur, and we need to plan ways to deal with those bumps. Things like changes in senior leadership, cuts in resources, the engagement of new or different stakeholders, the addition or loss of project members, and even students who just do not want to cooperate can all be unexpected conditions of implementing ePortfolios. During these moments, remember why you decided to turn to ePortfolios in the first place and to keep in mind the transformative potential that they offer to all stakeholders but especially for our learners. Lastly, please remember that you are not alone. There is a rich and vibrant community of ePortfolio users, instructors, staff, scholars, and researchers who have been in your shoes, with whom you can share experiences and ask questions, and, of course, who can commiserate with you, reassure you, and inspire you. Most important, the community is a place to share your challenges and successes, and we look forward to welcoming and engaging you in this ongoing conversation around ePortfolios and learning.

References

Ames, C., and Archer, J. 1988. "Achievement Goals in the Classroom: Students' Learning Strategies and Motivation Processes." *Journal of Educational Psychology* 80(3): 260–267.

Anderson, L. W., Krathwohl, D. R., et al., eds. 2000. *A Taxonomy for Learning, Teaching, and Assessing: A Revision of Bloom's Taxonomy of Educational Objectives*. Boston: Allyn & Bacon.

Arum, R., and Roksa, J. 2011. *Academically Adrift: Limited Learning on College Campuses*. Chicago: University of Chicago Press.

Association of American Colleges and Universities. 2011. *The LEAP Vision for Learning: Outcomes, Practices, Impact, and Employers' Views*. Washington, DC: Association of Ameriecan Colleges and Universities.

Barrett, H. 2004. "Electronic Portfolios as Digital Stories of Deep Learning: Emerging Digital Tools to Support Reflection in Learner-Centered Portfolios." http:// electronicportfolios.com/digistory/epstory.html.

Barrett, H. 2006. "Researching and Evaluating Digital Storytelling as a Deep Learning Tool." In *Proceedings of Society for Information Technology & Teacher Education International Conference 2006*, edited by C. Crawford et al., 647–654. Chesapeake, VA: AACE.

Batson, T., and Watson, C. E. February 2, 2011. "The Student Portfolio Is the New Book: New Practices, Profession, and Scholarship." *Campus Technology*. http:// campustechnology.com/articles/2011/02/02/the-student-portfolio-is-the-new-book .aspx.

Baxter Magolda, M. 2004. "Self-Authorship as the Common Goal of 21st-Century Education." In *Learning Partnerships: Theory and Models of Practice to Educate for Self-Authorship*, edited by M. Baxter-Magolda and Patricia King, 1–36. Sterling, VA: Stylus.

Baxter Magolda, M., and King, P. 2004. *Learning Partnerships: Theory and Models of Practice to Educate for Self-Authorship*. Sterling, VA: Stylus.

Biggs, J. 1987. *Student Approaches to Learning and Studying*. Hawthorn, VIC: Australian Council for Educational Research.

Biggs, J., and Tang, C. 2007. *Teaching for Quality Learning at University: What the Student Does (3rd Edition)*. Berkshire, England: Society for Research into Higher Education and Open University Press.

Bloom, B. S., ed. 1956. *Taxonomy of Educational Objectives: The Classification of Educational Goals, by a Committee of College and University Examiners. Handbook I: Cognitive Domain*. New York: Longmans, Green.

Brown, G., Peterson, N., Wilson, A., and Ptaszynski, J. 2008. "Out of the Classroom and Beyond." *Innovate* 4(5). http://www.innovateonline.info/index.php?view=article&id=559.

Brumm, T. J., Mickelson, S. K., and White, P. N. 2006. "Integrating Behavioral-Based Interviewing into the Curricula." *National Association of College Teachers in Agriculture (NACTA) Journal* 50(2): 28–31.

Cambridge, D. 2010. *Eportfolios for Lifelong Learning and Assessment*. San Francisco: Jossey-Bass.

Cambridge, D. et al. 2008. *INCEPR Final Report*, George Mason University. http://ncepr.org/finalreports/cohort3/George%20Mason%20Final%20Report.pdf.

Cambridge, D., Cambridge, B., and Yancey, K. (eds.). 2009. *Electronic Portfolios 2.0: Emergent Research on Implementation and Impact*. Sterling, VA: Stylus.

Chen, H. L. 2009. "Using ePortfolios to Support Lifelong and Lifewide Learning." In *Electronic Portfolios 2.0: Emergent Research on Implementation and Impact*, edited by Darren Cambridge, Barbara Cambridge, and Kathleen Yancey, 29–35. Sterling, VA: Stylus.

Chen, H. L., and Black, T. C. 2010 "Using E-Portfolios to Support an Undergraduate Learning Career: An Experiment with Academic Advising." *Educause Quarterly Magazine* 33(4). http://www.educause.edu/EDUCAUSE+Quarterly/EDUCAUSEQuarterlyMagazineVolum/UsingEPortfoliostoSupportanUnd/219102.

Chen, H. L., Cannon, D. M., Gabrio, J., and Leifer, L. 2005. "Using Wikis and Weblogs to Support Reflective Learning in an Introductory Engineering Design Course." *Proceedings of the American Society for Engineering Education Annual Conference and Exposition*, Portland, Oregon.

Chen, H. L., and Ittelson, J. C. 2009. "EPAC: Building a Community of Practice around e-portfolios." In *The Learning Portfolio*, edited by John Zubizarreta, 109–119. San Francisco: Jossey-Bass.

Chen, H. L., and Mazow, C. June 16, 2002. "Electronic Learning Portfolios in Student Affairs." *NetResults*. [This is an online publication available from http://www.naspa.org/pubs/mags/nr/default.cfm but is only available to NASPA members]

Chen, H. L., and Penny Light, T. 2010. *Electronic Portfolios and Student Success: Effectiveness, Efficiency, and Learning*, Washington. DC: Association of American Colleges and Universities.

Darcy, J., and M. Cuomo. July 20, 2010. *ePortfolio Cornerstone Community: Symphonic Reactions on Different Ways of Knowing.* Association of Authentic Experiential Evidence-Based Learning Annual Meeting.

Dewey, J. 1934. *Art as Experience.* New York: Penguin Books.

Digication. January 3, 2011. *SUNY Stony Brook University (SBU) Leverages Social Media to Promote and Celebrate Student Work and ePortfolios.* http://www.digication.com/blog/post:suny-stony-brook-university-sbu-leverages-social-media-to-promote-and-celebrate-student-work-and-eportfolios.

Dweck, C. S. 1986. "Motivational Processes Affecting Learning." *American Psychologist 41*: 1040–1048.

Educause. 2005. Educating the Net Generation. http://www.educause.edu/educatingthe netgen.

EPAC Community of Practice. 2011. ePortfolio-related Tools and Technologies. http://epac.pbworks.com/w/page/12559686/Evolving%20List%C2%A0of%C2%A0 ePortfolio-related%C2%A0Tools

Eynon, B. 2009a. "It Helped Me See a New Me": ePortfolio, Learning and Change at LaGuardia Community College. Academic Commons. http://www.academiccommons.org/files/Eynon_eportfolio_revised.pdf.

Eynon, B. 2009b. "Making Connections: The LaGuardia ePortfolio." In *Electronic Portfolios 2.0: Emergent Research on Implementation and Impact*, edited by Darren Cambridge, Barbara Cambridge, and Kathleen Yancey, 59–68. Sterling, VA: Stylus.

Fink, L. D. 2003. *Creating Significant Learning Experiences: An Integrated Approach to Designing College Courses.* San Francisco: Jossey-Bass.

Ford, C. et al. 2009. *Reactions to Curricular and Co-curricular Learning as Documented in an ePortfolio, Technical Report Number 48.* Florida State University. http://career.fsu.edu/techcenter/pdf/ncepr.pdf.

Garis, J. W. 2007. "ePortfolios: Concepts, Designs and Integration Within Student Affairs." In *Emerging ePortfolios: Opportunities for Student Affairs,* edited by J. W. Garis and J. Dalton. San Francisco: Jossey-Bass.

Garis, J. W., and Dalton J., eds. 2007. *Emerging ePortfolios: Opportunities for Student Affairs.* San Francisco: Jossey-Bass.

Griffin, J. E., Lorenz, G. F., and Mitchell, D. 2011. "A Study of Outcomes-Oriented Student Reflection During Internship: The Integrated, Coordinated, and Reflection Based Model of Learning and Experiential Education." *Journal of Cooperative Education & Internships 44*(2): 42–50.

Hart Research Associates. April 2009. *Learning and Assessment: Trends in Undergraduate Education—A Survey Among Members of the Association of American Colleges and Universities.* Washington, DC: Association of American Colleges and Universities.

Hart Research Associates. 2010. *Raising the Bar: Employers' Views on College Learning in the Wake of the Economic Downturn—A Survey Among Employers Conducted on Behalf of the Association of American Colleges and Universities*. Washington, DC: Association of American Colleges and Universities.

Hartmann, B., Klemmer, S. R., Bernstein, M., Abdulla, L., Burr, B., Robinson-Mosher, A., and Gee, J. October 15–18 2006. "Reflective Physical Prototyping Through Integrated Design, Test, and Analysis." In *ACM Symposium on User Interface Software and Technology (UIST)*, Montreux, Switzerland.

Hasso Plattner Institute of Design at Stanford. 2011. d.school Bootcamp Bootleg. http://dschool.stanford.edu/wp-content/uploads/2011/03/BootcampBootleg2010v2 SLIM.pdf.

The Henry J. Kaiser Family Foundation. 2010. *Generation M2: Media in the Lives of 8- to 18-Year-Olds*. http://www.kff.org/entmedia/mh012010pkg.cfm.

Huber, M., and P. Hutchings. 2004. *Integrative Learning: Mapping the Terrain*. Washington DC: Association of American Colleges and Universities.

Kallman, R., and Nguyen, C. F. February 2011. "Enhanced Electronic Transcript: The Electronic Portfolio for Learning and Achievement." *Pacific American Association of College Registrars and Admission Officers (PACRAO) Review* 1(1). https://sites.google .com/a/pacrao.org/pacrao-review/home/pacrao-review-archives-2011/2011-volume1-number1/2011v1n1-electronic-transcripts

Kamenetz, A. 2010. *DIY U*. White River Junction, VT: Chelsea Green Publishing.

Kelly, K. et al. 2010. "Mapping ePortfolio Artifacts to Objectives at Different Levels." ePortfolio Day of Dialogue, California State University. http://teachingcommons.cdl.edu/ eportfolio/resources/dop/mapping.html.

Kirkpatrick, J., Renner, T., Kanae, L., and Goya, K. 2009. "A Values-Driven Eportfolio Journey: Na Wa'a." In *Electronic Portfolios 2.0: Emergent Research on Implementation and Impact*, edited by D. Cambridge, B. Cambridge, and K. Yancey, 97–102. Sterling, VA: Stylus.

Kiser, P.M. 1998. "Integrative Processing Model: A Framework for Learning in the Field Experience." *Human Service Education* 18(1): 3–13.

Kuh, G. D. 2003. "What We're Learning About Student Engagement from NSSE: Benchmarks for Effective Educational Practice." *Change* 35(2): 24–32.

Kuh, G. D. et al. 2005. *Student Success in College: Creating Conditions That Matter*. San Francisco: Jossey-Bass.

Kuh, G. D. 2008. *High Impact Practices: What They Are, Who Has Access to Them, and Why They Matter*, Washington, DC: Association of American Colleges and Universities.

Leskes, A., and Miller, R. 2006. *Purposeful Pathways: Helping Students Achieve Key Learning Outcomes*. Washington, DC: Association of American Colleges and Universities.

Leskes, A., and Wright, B. D. 2005. *The Art and Science of Assessing General Education Outcomes: A Practical Guide*. Washington, DC: Association of American Colleges and Universities.

Lumina Foundation for Education. 2011. *The Degree Qualifications Profile*. http://www.luminafoundation.org/publications/The_Degree_Qualifications_Profile.pdf.

Mentkowski, M., and Associates. 2000. *Learning That Lasts: Integrating Learning, Development, and Performance in College and Beyond*. San Francisco: Jossey-Bass.

National Leadership Council for Liberal Education and America's Promise. 2007. *College Learning for the New Global Century*. Washington, DC: Association of American Colleges and Universities.

National Research Council. 2000. *How People Learn: Brain, Mind, Experience, and School: Expanding Research and Educational Practice, 2nd Edition*. Washington, DC: National Academy Press.

Norris, K. E., Price, M., and Steinberg, K. S. 2011. "Using Eportfolios to Enhance and Assess General Education and Civic Engagement: Challenges and Strategies." Presentation at the Association of American Colleges and Universities: General Education and Assessment Conference, Chicago.

Oblinger, D. 2003. "Boomers, Gen-Xers and Millennials: Understanding the New Students." *EDUCAUSE Review 38*(4): 37–47. http://www.educause.edu/ir/library/pdf/erm0342.pdf.

Osborne, K. 1991. *Teaching for Democratic Citizenship*. Toronto: Our Schools/Our Selves Education Foundation.

Peet, M., Lonn, S., Gurin, P., Boyer, K. P., Matney, M., Marra, T., Taylor, S. M., and Daley, A. 2011. "Fostering Integrative Knowledge Through ePortfolios." *International Journal of ePortfolio 1*(1): 11–31.

Penny Light, T. 2008. "Making Connections: Developing Students' Historical Thinking with Electronic Portfolios," *Academic Intersections 2*.

Pew Research Center. February 24, 2010. *The Millennials: Confident. Connected. Open to Change*. http://pewresearch.org/millennials/.

Prensky, M. 2001. *Digital Natives, Digital Immigrants*. http://www.marcprensky.com/writing/Prensky%20-%20Digital%20Natives,%20Digital%20Immigrants%20-%20Part1.pdf.

Ramsden, P. 2003. *Learning to Teach in Higher Education*. London: Routledge.

Reese, M., and Levy, R. 2009. *Assessing the Future: E-Portfolio Trends, Uses, and Options in Higher Education*. Boulder, CO: EDUCAUSE Center for Applied Research.

Rhodes, T., ed. 2010. *Assessing Outcomes and Improving Achievement: Tips and Tools for Using Rubrics*. Washington, DC: Association of American Colleges and Universities.

Rickards, W. H., and Guilbault, L. 2009. "Studying Student Reflection in an Electronic Portfolio Environment: An Inquiry in the Context of Practice." In *Electronic Portfolios 2.0: Emergent Research on Implementation and Impact*, edited by Darren Cambridge, Barbara Cambridge, and Kathleen Yancey, 17–28, Sterling, VA: Stylus.

Rodgers, C. 2002. "Defining Reflection: Another Look at John Dewey and Reflective Thinking." *Teachers College Record 104*(4): 842–866.

Saroyan, A., and Amundsen, C. 2004. *Rethinking Teaching in Higher Education: From a Course Design Workshop to a Faculty Development Framework.* Sterling, VA: Stylus.

Shada, A. 2011. *Electronic Portfolio Implementation in the Metro Academies Program at San Francisco State University and City College of San Francisco.* Unpublished master's thesis. Mills College, Oakland, California.

Shulman, L. 1998. "Teacher Portfolios: A Theoretical Activity." In *With Portfolio in Hand: Validating the New Teacher Professionalism*, edited by N. Lyons, 23–37. New York: Teachers College Press.

Social Science Research Council. 2011. *Learning in Higher Education: Core Findings*, http://highered.ssrc.org/?page_id=33.

Tosh, D., Werdmuller, B. Chen, H. L., Penny Light, T., and Haywood, J. 2006. "The Learning Landscape: A Conceptual Framework for ePortfolios." In *Handbook of Research on ePortfolios*, edited by A. Jafari and C. Kaufman, 24–32. London: IDEA Group Reference.

Trigwell, K., Prosser, M., and Waterhouse, F. 1997. "Relations Between Teachers' Approaches to Teaching and Students' Approaches to Learning." *Higher Education* 37(1): 57–70.

Venezky, R. L. 2001. "Procedures for Evaluating the Impact of Complex Educational Interventions." *Journal of Science Education and Technology* 10(1): 17–30.

Yancey, K. B. 1998. *Reflection in the Writing Classroom.* Logan: Utah State University Press.

Williams, B. T. 2007. "I'm Ready for My Close-Up Now: Electronic Portfolios and How We Read Identity." *Journal of Adolescent & Adult Literacy* 50(6): 500–504.

Zaldivar, M. 2011. "ePortfolios: Balancing Goals and Functionality." Virginia Tech.

Index

Q

Queensborough Community College's reflection cycle, 79–80

R

Radical Collaboration mindset, 30, 34–35

Ramsden, P., 7

Reese, M., 26, 34

Reflection: folio thinking and, 8–9, 10–11; identity development and, 11–18; importance of, 9–10; prompts, 56, 78

Reflection, modeling: necessity for, 76, 77; Queensborough Community College's reflection cycle, 79–80; taboo phrases for, 81–84

Research projects, ePortfolios that document, 58–59

Rhodes, T., 62, 99

Rickards, W. H. 146

Rodgers, C., 57

Roksa, J., 63, 146

Rubrics for evaluating ePortfolios, 2, 61–63, 98–103

S

Salt Lake Community College, "ePortfolios for Success" course at, 130

San Francisco State University (SFSU): eFolio tool used at, 126; Master of Public Health ePortfolio, 126, 127; stakeholder analysis at, 34, 35; support resources at, 130; web site accompanying this book and, 146

Security, plagiarism, and storage issues, 132–133

Self-authorship: defined, 12–13; as important skill, 11

SERVE (Students Engaging and Responding through Volunteer Experiences) program at Virginia Tech, 60, 89

Service learning and community-based learning, 59

Sexual ethics e-portfolio, example of, 13, 14, 15

Shada, A., 34

Show Don't Tell mindset, 30, 35–38

Shulman, L., 78

Significant learning experiences, 41, 42, 145

Situation Task Result (STAR) approach, 102–103

Sixth decade plan at University of Waterloo, 109

Skills journals, 100–102

Social networking sites: as links embedded within ePortfolios, 136; students' social identity and, 16

Staff, as stakeholders, 28

Stakeholders, ePortfolio: constellation of possible, 27; description of, 28; identifying, 2, 25, 26–29, 43, 51–52, 147; Implementation Framework adapted to, 1–4, 139, 146–148; selection of tools and, 137; Standford d.school's mindsets and, 26, 29–40

Stanford d.school, mindsets developed by, 26, 29–40

Stanford University's enhanced electronic transcript, 91–92

Steinberg, K. S., 87

Student affairs: benefits of ePortfolios for, 20–21; as stakeholders, 28

Student buy-in: "cabinet of curiosities" for, 73–75; fostering, 69; model ePortfolios for, 76, 77–78; reflection cycle for, 76, 79–80; strategies for framing ePortfolios and, 71–73; student consultants and, 75–76; students' perceptions of ePortfolios and, 70–71; taboo phrases of reflection and, 81–84

Students: benefits of ePortfolios for, 18, 19, 69; as self-authors, 13; as stakeholders, 28, 67; understanding, 43, 49–51, 70–71

SUNY Stony Brook's ePortfolio initiative, 75–76, 77–78

T

Taboo phrases of reflection, 81–84

Tamang, S., 77

Tang, C., 7

Tools to support ePortfolio implementation: implications for selection of, 137; important considerations for, 138; integration with course/learning management system and, 128–129; interoperability and, 131–132; key reasons for using, 123–125; student assessment needs and, 133–135; student control and, 126–128; support resources and, 129–131; usability of, 125–126